HOPS

Oregon State University Press CORVALLIS

HOPS

Historic Photographs *of the* Oregon Hopscape   KENNETH I. HELPHAND

The Oregon Hop Growers Association provided generous support that
helped make publication of this book possible.

Library of Congress Cataloging-in-Publication Data

Names: Helphand, Kenneth I., author.
Title: Hops : historic photographs of the Oregon hopscape / Kenneth I. Helphand.
Description: Corvallis : Oregon State University Press, 2020. | Includes
    bibliographical references.
Identifiers: LCCN 2020029155 | ISBN 9780870710179 (trade paperback)
Subjects: LCSH: Hops—Oregon—History.
Classification: LCC SB317.H64 H45 2020 | DDC 633.8/209795—dc23
LC record available at https://lccn.loc.gov/2020029155

∞ This paper meets the requirements of ANSI/NISO Z39.48-1992
(Permanence of Paper).

First published in 2020 by Oregon State University Press
Printed in Korea

Photograph on pages ii and iii: Panorama of the Zoller Hopyard, Mission Bottom,
Salem, 1913. Source: Zoller Hop Company Records (MSS Zoller), OSU Special
Collections and Archives Research Center, Corvallis, Oregon; Bush House
Museum, Salem Art Association, oregondigital_fx71cz66z.

Oregon State University Press
121 The Valley Library
Corvallis OR 97331-4501
541-737-3166 • fax 541-737-3170
www.osupress.oregonstate.edu

For my teachers, colleagues, and students who inspired a lifetime of learning

CONTENTS

PREFACE

I moved to Oregon in 1974 to begin teaching landscape architecture at the University of Oregon. Driving and biking in the Willamette Valley was how I first encountered the landscape of hops production. It was unlike any other agricultural environment I had ever witnessed. I was fascinated by the lines of poles, the lattice of wires, and the density of green growth. Many years later I decided to explore what I had seen and researched and wrote an article, "Grids and Garlands: The Landscape of Hops," for *SiteLines*, a landscape publication. In the course of doing that research, I was pleased and surprised to discover that the Oregon Hops and Brewing Archives (OHBA) was located a short drive away at Oregon State University in Corvallis. Looking through the archive, I encountered an extraordinary collection of photographs—not only significant historical documents but also images of exceptional quality—which inspired this book.

My goal in *Hops: Historic Photographs of the Oregon Hopscape* is to share those images and others that I have collected with a broader public. My initial interest was to understand how the hops landscape is constructed and its role in the agricultural landscape. However, I soon discovered that there was another significant story: how Oregonians were engaged in hop production and how the harvest of hops involved thousands of individuals.

Research began in the archives in Corvallis, but it took me to other historical archives in western Oregon where hops have been grown. I am grateful to the individuals and companies who have donated their materials to these institutions and to the archivists and volunteers at those institutions. I offer thanks to Scott Daniels and Robert Warren at the Oregon Historical Society, Joan Momsen at the Josephine County Historical Society, Carly Annable at the Independence Heritage Museum, Cheryl Roffe at Lane County History Museum, and archivists at the Polk County Historical Museum and Grants Pass Historical Society. Thomas Robinson's unique historical photographic archive provided wonderful images. Many other individuals have been helpful with information or as readers: Bob Jackson and Charlotte Helmer of Eugene; Steve Schreiber and Kimberlee Henkel-Moody; and Zak Schroerlucke, Anne Iskra, and Bradley Barnette at Crosby Hop Farm, who shared their experience and helped me understand the annual cycle of production. I gathered useful information online from Panhandle Forest Products, Kerr Supply Company, Hop Growers of America, and other sources. Peter Kopp's superb book *Hoptopia: A World of Agriculture and Beer in Oregon's Willamette Valley* provided a significant starting point.

At the Oregon State University Press I appreciate the initial enthusiasm, support, and encouragement for the project from Mary Elizabeth Braun and Tom Booth. Kim Hogeland has been my primary contact at the press. She has been a diligent editor, assisting in responding to anonymous reviewer comments and offering her own superb editorial advice. Erin Kirk provided a spectacular design for the book. Micki Reaman's diligent copyediting vastly improved the text. My sincerest thanks go to Tiah Edmunson-Morton, the librarian/archivist of the OHBA from its inception in 1993. From the outset she has given generously of her enormous knowledge about the world of hops, has connected me with resources and individuals and helped me make sure that I have done justice to the story of hops in Oregon.

Michelle Palacios, administrator of both the Oregon Hop Commission and the Oregon Hop Growers Association, connected me with the Oregon Hop Growers Association (OHGA). I made a presentation to the OHGA soliciting their support to ensure that this would be a publication that would be printed to the highest standards and do justice to the photographic record. I am most grateful for their support in ensuring the quality of this publication.

HOPS: PLANTS, PLACE, AND PEOPLE

"How is it?" she asked. "It's too hoppy," he said. "Try this one, it's not as bitter." "I prefer a maltier beer," she replied. The beer drinkers in the microbrewery were talking about hops. Many people enjoy the beverage, but few drinkers are knowledgeable about either the plant or the striking landscape where hops are grown, despite the presence of hopyards in the Pacific Northwest.

What are hops? The Latin name is *Humulus lupulus*—"wolf of the woods." Hops are a climbing perennial plant; the Latin name suggests its voracious twisting growth of up to twenty-five feet per year. Dioecious with separate male and female plants, the plant's female flower, also called the cone, is cultivated, with a male plant needed for pollination. Lupalin, an oily resin, is found inside the cone. This yellow substance provides the aroma and distinctive flavor in beer or ale.

THE JOURNEY TO OREGON

Hops have been cultivated since the eighth century and used in brewing for a millennium. They were first grown in Germany, which is still the world's largest hops producer. Around 1150 the Benedictine nun Hildegard von Bingen urged the inclusion of hops in beer as a preservative. In 1516 the Bavarian purity law (Reinheitsgebot) stated that barley, hops, and water would be the only ingredients allowed in brewing beer.

Flemish immigrants introduced hops to England in 1525. Kent, in Southern England, which now grows less than 2 percent of the world's hops, was the center of production until the early twentieth century. This international heritage is often reflected in modern hop terminology; the American hop dryer, for example, is called an oast house in England, based on a sixteenth-century Dutch term.

In the United States hops have been grown in all parts of the country. Hops were grown in the British colonies since 1629, but only in the nineteenth century did they reach prominence in the United States, first in Massachusetts, then Vermont, followed by New York State, as German immigrants brought their brewing skills. New York remained the center of production from the 1840s until it was superseded by California later in the century. By 1902 Oregon was leading all states in production of hops and remained so in most years until it was overtaken by Washington State in 1943.

The Willamette Valley offered ideal conditions for the cultivation of hops, including well-drained soil in the valley's alluvial bottomlands. One of the endpoints of the Oregon Trail, the valley had been characterized as a new Garden of Eden, with rich soils, water resources, river transportation, timber, and an amenable climate. The seasonal winter rain, a hard freeze that allows bines to die back, and a dry summer were all favorable growing conditions and similar to those found in Germany. The first documentation of hops in the Oregon Territory was in the 1850 census, noting a production of eight pounds. A decade later, after statehood, production was listed at 493 pounds. Although the same census noted only a single brewer in the state, at least two had opened since 1850: Englishman Charles Barret opened a brewery in Portland in 1854 and Henry Saxer, who immigrated from Switzerland, opened Liberty Brewery in 1856. Along with German immigrants, Barret and Saxer would be the state's pioneering brewers and hop growers.

Adam Weisner brought European rootstock to Oregon in 1867, having obtained it from a Wisconsin farmer, and with William Wells planted the first hops in Buena Vista, Polk County. However, their enterprise failed commercially. George Leasure's hopyard near Eugene yielded the first successful hop harvest in 1869. Later, the Seavey family enterprise rose to prominence in the southern Willamette Valley; they eventually extended their holdings north. In the 1880s Oregon production boomed, aided by the distribution possibilities of the Oregon and California Railroad, which reached Salem in 1870 and Eugene the following year, linking the valley to national markets. The first hopyards were in Lane County, but the center of cultivation soon moved north near Salem and Independence in Marion and Polk Counties, with another group of hopyards near Grants Pass. An 1887 article in the *West Shore*, a booster magazine and Oregon's first illustrated publication, touted the agricultural virtues of the Willamette Valley: "There is another profitable crop, to

which more attention is being paid yearly. No less than four hundred acres of hops are now growing within the limits of Polk County."

In 1898 the Oregon State Board of Agriculture declared that "the garden spot of the world for the cultivation of hops is the Willamette Valley," with Salem as the epicenter of the district. A Lane County Hop Growers Association was established in 1877 and in 1899 growers from eight counties formed the Oregon Hop Growers Association. The 1905 Lewis and Clark Exposition in Portland helped introduce Oregon hops to the world. Hops began as a secondary crop in the valley, but it ultimately became a significant force occupying thousands of acres. By the early twentieth century there were almost fifteen hundred growers, and Oregon rivaled Germany as the global center of production. Between 1920 and 1930 Oregon produced half of the hops in the United States on seventeen thousand acres. It was during this period that the valley became the self-styled "hops center of the world."

This period also saw the rise of Prohibition. As expected, hop growers vigorously lobbied against it. Yet while the Eighteenth Amendment in 1917 banned the production, importation, transportation, and sale of alcoholic beverages, growers continued to export their product to fill demand in Germany and Austria, still recovering from the effects of World War I and the downy mildew disease, which had destroyed crops there. Production increased after the end of Prohibition in 1935, but by the 1950s downy mildew had struck Oregon and obliterated most hopyards, a major contributing factor to the decline of production in Oregon. In addition, the much drier conditions in Washington's Yakima Valley were more advantageous for hop growth and downy mildew was not a problem there. By 1980 there were only five thousand acres of Oregon hops, a decline from almost twenty-two thousand in 1909. Additionally, the mechanization of picking in the 1950s led to the loss of many smaller hop farms, as farmers could not compete economically with larger growers. In 1949, there were over four hundred hop growers in the state of Oregon; by 1981 there were only forty. Despite these fluctuations in the hop industry, some Willamette Valley hopyards have stayed in the same family for three to four generations of continuous production. Goschie Farms near Silverton has been in production since 1904. Albert Crosby planted hops in 1900 and his farm is now in its fifth generation in Marion County.

American commercial production is still centered in the Pacific Northwest, with 98 percent of American hops grown there: in 2018 there were 55,035 acres under cultivation, producing 107 million pounds of hops. The Yakima Valley grows 75 percent of hops produced in the United States, with the rest almost equally divided between Oregon and Idaho. In 2015 the United States surpassed Germany as the world's leader. The success of the craft brewing industry and the demand for a hoppier beer have led to a resurgence in the demand for hops. Microbrewing and home brewing have encouraged growers throughout the nation. Oregon's first craft brewery was established in 1980 and the first brew pub, a McMenamins, opened in 1985. In 2017 there were over six thousand craft breweries and brew pubs in the country, an almost 200 percent increase in five years, and the trajectory continues upward.

THE HOPS LANDSCAPE

Agricultural landscapes are the visible evidence of the craft of agriculture, the honed and artful skill employed to ensure the best production. Crops such as grapes, tree fruits, and hops are grown in such visibly handcrafted landscapes. The geographer John Fraser Hart notes that all forms of agriculture are ordering systems that create a characteristic "look of the land." The marriage of plants, manual skill, and tools (hand or mechanical) creates landscapes based on the pragmatic requirements of agriculture. Each agricultural activity leaves an imprint on the land; some are relatively permanent, like field patterns, orchard grids, irrigation channels, and terracing, while others reflect the ephemerality of the seasonal cycle of agricultural activity from planting through harvest. This year-round activity creates patterns, forms, and spaces in the landscape that are aesthetically pleasing. This is the "art" of agriculture, of which hops are a prime example.

Hops are grown in hopyards, the term for a field of hops; other common terms include hop farms and hop ranches. Hopyards vary in scale from small domestic yards of less than an acre to commercial enterprises of over four hundred acres. Hopyards are immediately recognizable by a regular grid of poles and trellises, the structures that support the stringing of hops and the growth of the plants. The unique appearance of hopyards is the consequence of dramatic construction of the architecture of agriculture, an "agritecture." Agritecture includes all small-scale elements that support or protect growing plants: stakes for beans and tomatoes, arbors for grapes, posts supporting sagging apple branches, cloches and nets covering growing plants. The large scale and scope of the poles, wires, twine, and stakes hopyards use presents one of the most recognizable examples of agritecture.

A hopyard represents a substantial economic investment. As Michael Tolman, author of *Tinged with Gold: Hop Culture in the United States*, notes, the up-front costs include "preparing the soil; manuring, cultivating, and laying out the fields; setting the roots; procuring poles, wires, twine, and burlap; obtaining dusting and baling equipment, picking baskets, boxes, and sacks; and building a kiln." Even before planting, a hopyard must be established, actually constructed, and the land prepared for production. Only then can the agricultural and seasonal cycle commence. The first step is the selection of a site. A flat or slightly sloping, well-drained site with a southerly orientation is ideal. The prime soil conditions for hops are a sandy loam characteristic of the bottomlands of the Willamette Valley.

The next step in establishing a hopyard is building a trellis, poles with wires attached to support the growing plants. The geometric spacing of the poles and plants should be designed to maximize yield, thwart disease, ease the task of harvest, and create a microclimate favorable to production. Contemporary yards are laid out in a straight regular grid of poles spaced about twenty-five feet apart, and rows of poles are commonly fourteen feet apart. The distance between poles is determined by the profusion of the bine's growth and the space required

to allow the passage of workers and machines through the yard. Hop plants or "hills" are spaced three and a half feet apart, equaling almost nine hundred plants per acre (although this has varied between six hundred and one thousand hills per acre). An orientation with the main support wires running east–west and the trellis wires north–south gives the best exposure, which allows the most penetration of the sun to the growing plants. Hops need fifteen hours of sunlight during their growing season and the long summer days in the Northwest are ideal. The ultimate result is a dramatic trellised landscape, a three-dimensional green grid.

Before the introduction of trellises and the accompanying wirework, poles were set atop small mounds of planted hops. England was the historical center of hops production, and while the acreage has dramatically declined, poles still retain a hold on the English imagination and are part of the lore of hops. English agricultural literature was replete with advice on proper practice that was followed for centuries. Thomas Tusser's 1573 *Five Hundred Points of Good Husbandry* advised three poles per hillock, planted "as straight as a leveled line of the hand." Reynolde Scot's 1574 treatise, *A Perfite Platform of a Hoppe Garden,* advised three to four alder poles fifteen to sixteen feet high on each hill, with hills planted nine to ten feet apart. Eighteenth-century English agricultural writer William Marshall described poling as "one of the nicest operations in hop cultivation—perhaps because of the aesthetic pleasure of setting poles on the carefully aligned hills and admiring the symmetry that resulted." In 1883 Ezra Meeker, author of the widely read book of advice, *Hop Culture in the United States,*

Hop mound, Kent

SOURCE: Reynolde Scot, *A Perfite Platform of a Hoppe Garden*, 1574

and the first of several individuals who would be anointed as the "Hop King," was still advocating a traditional poling system with one pole per hill of hops set seven feet apart and arranged in a square pattern. In the early twentieth century, trellises—wiring systems supported by poles—gradually replaced traditional poling. Trellises made harvesting easier and despite the added cost of wire, the need for fewer poles meant a substantial cost saving. However, poles remain the largest single cost, besides land, in establishing the infrastructure of the hopyard.

The hops grower employs a mathematics and a geometry to developing a hopyard. Variables that enter into the calculation include the choice of pole size, wood type, and the spacing between poles; these variables depend on the variety of hops that are grown, soil type, and weather conditions. Sixteen to eighteen feet is the most common height for contemporary poles, although they can vary from fourteen to twenty-five feet and are between three and seven inches in diameter—taller poles are wider. Post holes are dug to a depth of three to four feet and the poles encased in cement. Douglas fir and the longer-lasting cedar are preferred for poles in the Pacific Northwest, lodgepole pine as well as larch and locust in the East. Poles must be sturdy and firmly anchored to support the wires and ultimately the weight of the growing plant. Surrounding the perimeter of every hopyard are angled poles that are anchored and clamped, stabilizing and keeping the overhead wires in tension. A stay pole at the end of each row, a "dead man," braces the wires. The grid of the upright narrow poles recalls the columns of a building in the early stage of construction, awaiting the attachment of wires as the lines of poles diminish toward a vanishing point.

In a quest for the greatest efficiency and economic viability, growers have experimented with many poling systems over the years. In the umbrella system, wires are trained in symmetrical triangles between poles. The effect is passages beneath continuous series of green, pointed arches. In the Butcher system, wires are strung from lower to upper cross wires. A walk between furrows is as if the hops are one half of a sloping green roof. One little-used system enabled harvest at a level where hops could be strung and picked by a standing worker. The horizontal hop system, a high wire trellis with tall poles connected by wires with string attached to the overhead wires, eventually became most popular and still dominates hop-yards. Developers of harvesting machinery adapted it to the dimensions of the furrow.

GROWING HOPS

Hops are a perennial and they sprout after a winter dormancy. The hop plant can be propagated in a greenhouse, but more often they are planted from rootstock from the previous year's growth. In late winter and early spring rhizomes are dug from the dormant plant to be replanted. These hops cuttings are planted in small hills, allowing sufficient light and air for the growing plant. Ezra Meeker suggested three to five cuttings per hill, with one male plant per hundred hills needed to impregnate the female plants.

Hop growing is a labor-intensive enterprise. Once poles are in place, the ground between the furrows is plowed, throwing the earth away from the rootstock. The next step is the stringing of the yard. A single acre can be entwined with over a mile of cable, ultimately supporting up to twenty tons of hops. In current practice wires are strung at right angles between poles, and on one acre there can be between seventy-five and over three hundred poles. Stringing wires to posts is technical and laborious. The main cross or guy wires link the poles at a height of fifteen to eighteen feet. Wires are typically strung diagonally, ultimately creating green V's or U's of climbing plants. One criterion for trellis layout is the pickability of the crop, the "pluckability" that ensures less breakage of the cones. In early spring twining crews ride through the hopyards on raised platforms, now drawn by tractors but previously horse

drawn. Stringers drop lines of twine that are tied to the trellis wire at one end and then tautly staked at the base of each plant. The numbers and labor are daunting, with 1,500–3,500 strings per acre. For example, Rogue Farms in Independence now uses 78,788 individually hand-tied strings on its fifty-two-acre farm.

Before the end of winter, fields are plowed and hoed. Bines appear from the hop root (crown) and from these a few promising bines are chosen. Each hill will yield a plant that will be individually wound in a clockwise direction around the tautly staked string, with three to four bines per pole. Unwanted runners, early hop shoots that are not trained, are grubbed out and pruned by hand and hoe. The *Grants Pass Daily Courier* (May 9, 1937) reported that

> a string saver's paradise might be one of the numerous hop yards in Josephine County. The King and Eismann yards show a veritable forest of twine string that greets the observer after a crew has strung the twine for each hop plant in the score of acres. After strings are up, crews go through the yards training each plant onto the string, choosing only one or two sturdy shoots to wind about the string—and it will wind only one certain way. The rest of the shoots are cut away.

The twine, known as coir, is made from the fiber of coconut husks, a coarse fiber the hop tendrils, which have sharp hooks, easily grasp. Planters have also used twine from treated paper. Amazingly efficient workers can ambidextrously tie the strings as they ride through the yard. In an earlier era perhaps the most picturesque of rural crafts was workers stringing hops while marching through the yard on stilts. Noncommercial trellises can be strung in any form, limited only by imagination. There are trellises in the shape of flagpoles, cobwebs, clotheslines, arbors, or arboreal yurts.

With each stage in the seasonal cycle, hopyards go through dramatic changes. In the spring the yard is a field of poles and wires. As the bines mature, they are trained on the wire. In May the sprouts are about three feet long and are tied around the twine by hand. In Britain this is also known as "twiddling." During summer, the yards are weeded, sprayed, and pruned. By late summer, the hops have wound up the twine and across the strings connecting the columnar poles. As they reach the trellis cross wire, the hops are trained for the final time. Leaves are stripped about five feet from the ground, encouraging the strength of plant growth toward the top bines. By fall the bines cover the hopyard in a dense green blanket, their weight creating a canopy of hops. This shades the ground and grubbing—digging into the earth to remove weeds—is no longer needed; little plowing or harrowing needs to be done until harvest.

Growers are always on a quest for resistant varieties, because hops are susceptible to a variety of plant diseases (hop mold, or downy mildew, is a particular problem) and insect pests, including spider mites and aphids. To combat both, hopyards are dusted or sprayed. Spraying was historically done with a mixture of quassia chip—natural insecticide from a tree native to South America and the Caribbean—and whale oil soap, as well as a mixture of copper sulphate and quick lime. Cyanamide was used against the blight of downy mildew. Growers vigilantly observed its spread and pulled any affected spikes and shoots as soon as the disease manifested itself. At one time DDT was in common usage, but now safer chemical methods are employed. Al Hansen, whose family founded a hopyard in 1925, said spraying on his farm would start in July. "The sprayer was pulled at first with a team of horses and had a gas meter to pump pressure and the two men would walk behind and spray the vines." Though commonly called vines, which attach to surfaces by suckers or tendrils, hops are technically bines. Bines climb by twisting around a support clockwise in helical fashion, much like DNA.

Little commercial fertilizing was done before 1930, as fields were manured. Now chemical fertilizers and especially ground limestone are added because hops need a nonacidic soil to thrive. Depending on their location, some fields have also been irrigated with earthen channels constructed in the fields.

THE HARVEST

Hopyards before harvest are a magnificent sight. The poles and wires disappear, shrouded by garlands of green. A walk down the furrows takes one along narrow passageways, fences of green bordering long corridors extending to the vanishing point. A 1901 article described a hopyard as a "forest of green vines," while a 1904 *Oregonian* article lauded the magnitude of the developing hop industry and, in a bit of scenic boosterism, noted:

Who can look at a yard in its golden beauty, when ripened, and ready for picking—its trellis wires 18 feet above the earth—its foliage draped in beauty from the wires above of the ground below—its vines covered with the perfect yellow of the many ripened hops—the rows as straight as the compass can make them—and the ground below pulverized until perfectly smooth, and not be impressed with the scenic grandeur before them.

Hops are ready for fall harvest in late August or early September. Picking is best at the moment of maturity and the grower determines the ideal moment when there is a maximum quantity of lupulin. The moment is different for each variety. Sophisticated chemical and sensory analyses are done in a laboratory, but there is no substitute for experience. Expertise has been passed down from one generation of hop growers to the next. Dried samples are taken in hand and rubbed and sniffed. While visiting the Crosby Hop Farm, I was told the simple formula: "Grab a cone, look at it, smell it, feel it." This is the final call.

Before the use of trellises, the poles were stripped and dismantled by pole men or pole pullers. A bottom cutter cut the bines near the ground and a top cutter did the same from above. These poles were then stacked as pyramids awaiting their use the following season. Ezra Meeker described this process as a somewhat "messy agriculture." Once the trellis system was in place other methods took over. Now a "wireman" cuts the bine, and the bines are moved to the mechanical picker, where the hops are stripped from the bine.

Taken from the bine, the ideal hop is a cone that is cleanly picked: unbroken and free of leaves, stems, bines, string, and dirt. "Dirty picking" was a perennial problem, and the best workers were known as "clean pickers." Many recall the powerful smell of hops and hearing the sound of "wire down" as the bines were pulled down for picking. Pickers were typically put into groups of fifty to sixty. The picked hops were placed in baskets, most often made of wooden slats, but also woven of camas and cloth. A basket held about 25 pounds. In 1909 an average worker could pick 80–125 pounds in a twelve-hour workday and an accomplished worker could pick 200 pounds of hops per day, and some even 400 pounds. Pickers took pride in their ability. In 1920 the Riggles twins attempted to break their record of twenty-seven picked boxes in a day.

When the baskets were full, pickers yelled "bags full," and they were emptied into sacks that held two baskets worth of hops. Kids used nail kegs or bushel baskets. Baskets were dumped into a hopper with a cloth-covered frame. When a sack of hops was full, the picker yelled "weigher" and the sack was weighed in the field by the weighmaster and scalesman. The picker was then given a tag with the weight. The weighmaster kept a duplicate that was checked when pickers were paid.

The distinctive architecture of hop farms and their yards includes drying houses—also called hop houses or drying kilns—with signature ventilating cupolas sprouting from their rooftops. These wooden buildings, with furnaces below, were always in danger of catching fire. At the drier, the sacks of green hops were unloaded onto the upper floors and laid two feet deep on slatted drying floors, allowing heated air from below to circulate. Fires in the kiln below, kept at 140 degrees, dried the green hops. At one time sulphur or saltpeter was burned to give the hops a uniform color. Once dry, a process that takes less than two days, hops were moved to a cooling room before being compressed into dense 200-pound bales for transport in the shape of giant sugar cubes.

An acre of hops produces twelve to twenty tons of biomass, which equals one ton of dried hops. Each acre yields about ten bales of dried hop cones, about two pounds per hill. Every four pounds of green hops yields one pound of dried hops. A bale will be used in brewing 135 to 800 barrels of beer (thirty-one gallons each), depending on the recipe.

THE PICKERS

Before mechanized picking, hops were harvested by hand by pickers, who were also known as hoppers. The harvest could last as long as a month and created a rich and incredibly diverse culture. Tens of thousands of pickers were needed for the three-week Oregon harvest. Anyone could pick hops, for it does not require great skill, although there were pickers who were more "professional" with "nimble fingers" who could pick "clean" and with speed. Hoppers included men, women, and children of all ages.

Large numbers of pickers came from near and far. Local residents walked, biked, rode to the fields in a horse and buggy and later by automobile, or were picked up by trucks. Many nearby towns were virtually empty during harvest-time. Steamboats brought pickers upriver from Portland to the hopyards. Others took the Oregon Electric Railway, the Southern Pacific—which put in extra couches—or boarded "Hop Special" trains much like the hopper trains that once brought workers from London to hopyards in Kent. Major growers like the Krebs Brothers and Horst Company even chartered their own trains from Portland.

Each group of pickers were seen to have different qualities in terms of speed, productivity, and reliability. In the nineteenth century few pickers were of European descent. In the Pacific Northwest the original pickers were Native Americans; some travelled by canoe from as far away as British Columbia to work in the hopyards. They were viewed as reliable workers and clean pickers but considered slow by the white growers. In later years Native Americans came from both the coast and the Siletz and Grand Ronde tribes and the Warm Spring Reservation into the Willamette Valley. Growers made space available for the Indians who arrived by horse and wagon and needed to pasture their animals.

The need for pickers depended on the vicissitudes of the market. In 1882 there was a worldwide hop shortage and getting enough pickers was difficult, but Chinese workers were readily available. Soon they were joined by Japanese and Filipino laborers. Reflecting the racial prejudice of the day, growers preferred "white" workers when they were available. In 1906 the *Oregonian* reported during a period of particularly heavy rain that "Hoppickers, especially white people, flatly balk at working under such conditions, but the Chinese and Japanese do not mind it so much."

There were Chinese hop growers in addition to hop pickers. The Tune Lee Chinese company leased ninety acres of the Krebs Brothers hopyard near Independence. After the 1882 Chinese Exclusion Act, Chinese were not permitted to enter the United States. The next year it was reported that "the crusaders continue to drive the Mongolians from Marion County hops yards." At a hopyard "leased to a Chinaman," shots were fired, "but no was hurt as the purpose was only to scare the Chinese away. It is certainly an assured fact that Chinamen will not pick many crops in Marion County this year and another year they will hardly venture to be in the way." To help meet the need for labor and to avoid employing Chinese, the Independence school system delayed the opening of school so children could join the harvest. This was not unusual; in many areas, schools were closed until the harvest was completed.

A 1913 *Oregonian* article in praise of manual labor, and surely written by an urbanite, declared that "hoppicking gives Oregonians that opportunity to return to the primitive that keeps us from over-civilizing." But picking was not all fun and was subject to heat, dust, flies, and tedium. Many pickers wore gloves or wrapped their hands with tape as protection from the prickly bines. Picking in the rain was difficult and too much rain lessened the grade of the hops. The sticky juice from the plant stained pickers' clothes. Pickers rose early, for payment was determined by weight: dew-laden hops weighed more than sun-dried hops.

In 1920 the *Oregonian* reported that thirty thousand pickers were beginning work September 1, in a year when the crop was half as large as previous years. That year wages were $1.50 per hundred pounds of picked hops, up thirty cents. Before the war, wages had been eight-five cents to $1.00 per hundred pounds. During the Depression, migrant workers and the unemployed worked as pickers. In the 1940s, Mexican laborers were imported as agricultural workers as part of the Bracero program. Nonwhite workers were often discriminated against and underpaid, but their labor was valued nonetheless. Beth Monroe of Independence recalled that she had "lots of Japanese friends" and "went to school with their kids, and they were just part of the community. There was no thought of discrimination against these people and, of course, these were our friends and we were a little horrified when they went into internment camps. 'Cause they were just part of us." There was such a shortage of laborers during World War II that soldiers from Camp Adair were drafted for the work in Oregon. In addition, German POWs held at Camp Adair were brought to the fields accompanied by a single guard and segregated into secure yards. Members of the Women's Land Army picked, as did Oregon State Agricultural College (now Oregon State University) co-eds who were drafted into the effort.

Bessie Down, who picked hops for almost thirty years starting at age eight, described how the small city of Independence overflowed at picking time. The numbers were large, up to fifty thousand pickers, at a time when the entire population of Polk County was just over fourteen thousand. By comparison contemporary hopyards employ one worker per fourteen to twenty acres in the spring and twice that at harvest time. Mechanical pickers equal the work previously done by about thirty workers. Manual picking dominated until after World War II and is still practiced in small hopyards, but the basic parameters began to change with the introduction of mechanical harvest machines that were designed to accommodate the dimensions of the furrows. Small growers could not afford

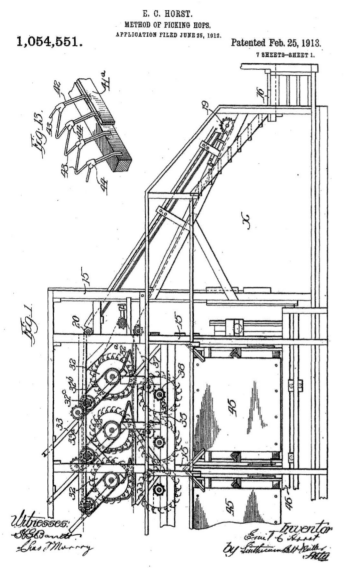

SOURCE: *Independence Monitor*, September 12, 1913

the expense and investment required for mechanical pickers; most turned to other forms of agriculture or other occupations. As one grower put it, at a certain point the choice was "either get big or get out."

SOCIAL LIFE IN THE HOP CAMPS

Picking was an unusual combination of work and a unique type of leisure and social environment. For most pickers, later in life it remained a pleasant memory of enjoyable outside work and a break from the everyday routine of their lives. There were formal and informal social occasions with music, campfires, gambling, weekend boxing and wrestling matches, evangelists, evening entertainment, and dances particularly popular. Some yards even showed movies in the evening and were visited by ice cream or Dutch oven pie vendors.

Pickers lived in camps that had sprung up during the fall harvest. Some growers provided housing but most common were tent encampments, which took on the trappings of temporary communities. Entire families camped in the countryside during harvest time, joining seasonal workers. In 1907 the Krebs Brothers Hop Ranch outside of Independence was the "Biggest Hopyard in the World." It advertised that it offered workers "perfect accommodations; grocery store, bakery, butcher shop, barber shop, dancing pavilion 50 x 150 feet, telephone, physician, beautiful camping ground; 3-acre bathing pool, restaurant, provisions sold at Portland prices. We pay $1.10 per 100 pounds; reduced excursion rate on our special trains." They had dances every night and on Sundays up to six thousand visitors came from the area and neighboring hopyards.

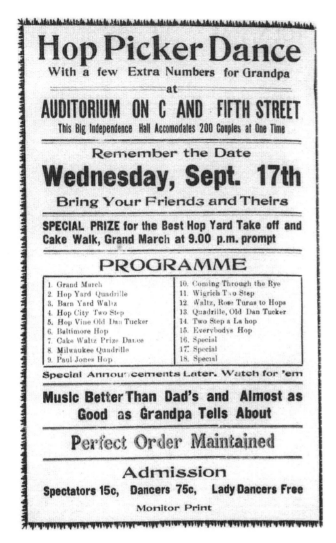

There could be problems with rowdy behavior amongst the pickers, so growers often preferred families. Hop picking brought together people from all walks of life, fostering a certain democratic spirit amongst the pickers despite their diverse motivations. Indian pickers, by choice or segregation, kept to their own villages and wove their own distinctive willow baskets for the harvest. Groups from the same town even organized their tents into named streets.

In the summer of 1907 pioneering sociologist Anne MacLean joined hop pickers in Oregon as a participant observer and focused on the poor conditions for women, a group that included shop girls, factory workers, waitresses, housewives, nurses, cooks, and students. MacLean's report was not all bleak; she also characterized the social mixture of pickers as "the democracy of the hop field." This was "hop time." Some considered the picking time to be a vacation, a picnic, outing, or "holiday time"; local high school kids considered it "summertime fun." For most it was certainly a respite from their conventional routines. It was not uncommon for couples to meet and even to marry in the hopyards. Marjorie Moshier met her "line man" husband of over sixty years at the end-of-season party, her "most precious memory" of the 1915 picking season at the Seavey yard in Springfield.

HOP FIESTA

Picked, dried, and baled: the hop harvest is complete. The bines have been pulled down, the poles remain, and on the wires remnants of string hang, looking like bits of tinsel. The ground, littered with bines, leaves, and string, awaits plowing and the planting of a cover crop. For the grower, work never ceases. Trellises are repaired and new ones installed; equipment is repaired. Planting a cover crop between the furrows, usually grass or a grain such as barley, is common practice. With the first killing frost the hops will go dormant, awaiting their natural cycle as a perennial plant to return in the spring.

Given their primary role as an ingredient in flavoring beer, it is not surprising that hops are also feted in festivals. The completion of a harvest is often followed by celebration and ritual. In 1927 Independence inaugurated an annual multiday "Hop Fiesta." The celebration included a parade, carnival, entertainment, dances, the crowning of a "hop queen," and evening fireworks. The popularity of the fiesta followed the vicissitudes of hop production; by the mid 1950s, it had waned and was not revived until the twenty-first century.

While hops are still celebrated, the celebration is now largely focused on the local community and its heritage. Along the Interstate 5 corridor that cuts through the Willamette Valley, there are few signs of hopyards. But take a trip off the highway and within a few miles, in the heart of the valley near Salem or Independence, hopyards appear. For those new to this stunning landscape, it is an unexpected experience. For those who follow the progress of the hopyards' seasonal transition from the striking grid of poles to a "forest of green vines," it is a never-ending delight.

REFERENCES

Davis, H. L. 1935. *Honey in the Horn*. New York: William Morrow, 1935.

Edwardson, John R. "Hops: Their Botany, History, Production and Utilization." *Economic Botany* 6 (April 1952):160–175.

Hieronymous, Stan. *For the Love of Hops: The Practical Guide to Aroma, Bitterness and the Culture of Hops*. Boulder, CO: Brewers Publications, 2012.

Joyce-Bulay, Catie. "A Year in the Life of a Hop." *OnTrak* (Spring 2018): 39–43.

Kopp, Peter. *Hoptopia*. Oakland: University of California Press, 2016.

Kopp, Peter A. "'Hop Fever' in the Willamette Valley: The Local and Global Roots of a Regional Specialty Crop." *Oregon Historical Quarterly* 112, no. 4 (Winter 2011): 406–433.

Kuhlman, G. W. and R. E. Fore. *Cost and Efficiency in Producing Hops in Oregon*. Corvallis, OR: Agricultural Experiment Station Bulletin 364, Oregon State College, 1939.

Larsen, Dennis. *Hop King: Ezra Meeker's Boom Years*. Pullman: Washington State University Press, 2016.

MacLean, Anne Marion. "With Oregon Hop Pickers." *American Journal of Sociology* 15, no. 1 (July 1909): 83–95.

Meeker, Ezra. *Hop Culture in the United States*. Puyallup, WA: Ezra Meeker & Co., 1883.

Myrick, Herbert. *The Hop*. Springfield , MA: Orange Judd Company, 1909.

Nelson, Herbert. "The Vanishing Hop-Driers of the Willamette Valley." *Oregon Historical Quarterly* 64, no. 3 (September 1963): 267–271.

Newton, Sidney. *Early History of Independence, Oregon*. Self-published, 1971.

Scot, Reynolde. *A Perfite Platform of a Hoppe Garden*. London: Henrie Denham, 1576.

Wilson, John M. *The Rural Cyclopedia: or A General Dictionary of Agriculture, and of the Arts, Sciences, Instruments, and Practice, necessary to the Farmer, etc.* Edinburgh: A. Fullarton and Co, 1852.

Tusser, Thomas. *A Hundreth Goode Pointes of Husbandrie.* 1557

Tomlan, Michael A. *Tinged with Gold: Hop Culture in the United States.* Athens: University of Georgia Press, 1992.

WEBSITES

http://www.schmidthops.com

http://www.greatlakeshops.com/hops

http://www.usahops.org/

https://www.brewersassociation.org

https://hopsdirect.com

YouTube: Hops TV @hopsdirect, 15 episodes

NEWSPAPERS

(Newspapers were accessed through Historic Oregon Newspapers: http://oregonnews.uoregon.edu)

Aurora Observer

Barrel and Box: Devoted to the Box, Cooperage, Pail, Stave, Headings & Hoop Interests (accessed through Google Books)

Hopper

Independence Enterprise

Independence Monitor

Independence West Sider

Newberg Graphic

Oregonian and *Sunday Oregonian*

Polk County Observer

Rogue River Courier (Grants Pass)

Stayton Mail

West Side Enterprise (Independence)

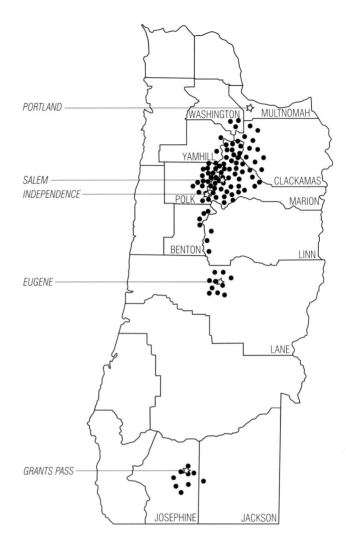

Distribution of hops in the Willamette and Rogue Valleys, 1930s.

Map design by Rebecca Cruz. SOURCE: G. W. Kuhlman and R. E. Fore, *Cost and Efficiency in Producing Hops in Oregon*, Agricultural Experiment Station Bulletin 364 (Corvallis: Oregon State College, 1939).

THE PHOTOGRAPHS

The two most common photographic subjects are people and places. In this collection almost all of the images combine both, a record of a history and culture. They also follow and document the agricultural process and activity of a hopyard through the seasons, from planting to harvest.

The people and places are captured either in a snapshot or candid fashion in the course of doing their labor, or in posed portraits of individuals or groups. Many photographs are environmental portraits: people in the setting of their activity, often accompanied by the tools of their labor or craft. The landscape "background" in the picture becomes a subject equal to the individuals in the foreground. In a sense the hopyard functions as the photographer's studio. In an era when painted backdrops were often used for formal portraits in a photographer's studio, the backdrop in these historical photographs is always out of doors with the poles and plants of the hopyard as the backdrop. Together they suggest a narrative.

The most common images are people working: constructing a trellis, hoeing, irrigating, stringing, picking, weighing, bagging or at the dryer. While static images, these are action shots capturing a moment in the process of growing and harvesting hops. While they show a single moment, they are documents of the repetitive work of tying a string, hoeing the ground, staking, twining a bine, picking the hop, hefting a bale. They also show and catalogue the tools and equipment: hoes, baskets, poles, wires, twine, and bales. They show the mechanisms of power: human muscle and horses, sprayers, wagons and later tractors, trucks and mechanical pickers. There are also images of people not at work, in the leisure time in the camps that was an integral part of the hop picker's experience.

The photographs of pickers are the most striking. Picking was a group activity, communal in nature. There are pictures of pairs of pickers, family groups, and ensembles of dozens of individuals, often of the crews pickers were assigned to. These group portraits invariably include men, women, and children as well as animals: horses and the inevitable dogs. The group photographs have a celebratory aspect as a permanent record of participation in that season's harvest. They have a kinship to photographs of school groups, army units, or the company picnic, marking the community that they were part of, even if only for the few weeks of summer picking season.

There are conventions to group photographs. Everyone's face should be visible. Look at the camera. Tall persons to the rear, short in the front, sitting or kneeling. People are lined up or stacked in ascending layers. Oftentimes there is social hierarchy, with the most important person, often the eldest, holding center stage. Most of these photographs conform to those conventions, but with critical variations. In a few photos a young man has climbed and is perched clinging to a pole overlooking the scene. All the included photographs depict the hopyard. Some are taken before harvest, perhaps as people arrived at the camp dressed up and not yet in their work clothes, with the still unharvested hops as the backdrop. In some, Native Americans are proudly showing off their traditional regalia. Other pictures were taken during the course of a harvest, with poles and wires down in the foreground and more work still to be done in the background. The photos communicate a pride in the work. In preparation for their work, stringers draped twine around their shoulders like huge scarfs. Some photos portray festive occasions, as pickers bedeck themselves with garlands of hops as headdresses. Everyone is wearing a hat; it is still summertime. Women are all in dresses until co-eds arrive in the 1940s. The hoppers' equipment—baskets, boxes, bags, bales, scales, or a wireman's pole—looks like the props for a theatrical performance. Most common, taking center stage, is a basket or bag full of hops prominently and proudly exhibited in the foreground.

Looking at the group photos, it is tempting to search for familiar faces, although few of us will know anyone in the picture. But you might imagine yourself as a kid sitting cross-legged for the picture, or as part of a family picking together.

These are photographic documents, an image archive, a collective chronicle of a landscape and culture that has largely disappeared. There is often the feeling that the photographer came upon people working in the hopyards, asked them to stop for a few moments for a picture, and they then returned to work. It is generally the growers who commissioned these images from professional photographers, and some were used for promotional purposes. In the 1930s Wigrich commissioned an annual album of photographs. The photographs by Dorothea Lange for the Farm Security Administration during the Depression were intended for national distribution to communicate the life of rural America across the nation. A few images document the work of agricultural researchers, many of whom had dual appointments at Oregon State University and the USDA. These crop scientists have conducted hop research since the 1890s. A few photos tell a whole hop story in a single image: the hopyard, pickers, bales being transported to the dryer, the dryer in the background. The experience was not all work, thus aspects of camp life are pictured as well. All generations are present from babies to grandparents. There are rural, small town, and city folk. Individuals who walked, rode, or came on horseback, train or steamboat. There are recent arrivals to the state with migrants working alongside those who came via the Oregon Trail. Collectively, the pickers were a microcosm of the state in this period: Chinese, Japanese, Native Americans, Armenians, Germans, Swedes, Mexicans, nuns, students, soldiers, and surely more unidentified groups of pickers.

There is an artistry to the photographs. A solitary man atop a platform repairing a wire, people in a vast sea of vegetation. There are dramatic compositions capturing the striking geometry of the enterprise: lines of poles to the vanishing point, grids of columns, lush corridors of hops, fields blanketing the ground, the mosaic pattern of bags and bales. There are stringers bedecked with twine, people aloft, the stringing dramatizing the verticality of the hopyard and the plants that can grow as high as a three-story building in a season.

There is an elegiac quality for a lost period and lost way of life. Hops are still grown now, but the process is more mechanized compared to a period when most labor was by hand. The number of individuals involved is much smaller. We now see the world in color and not in black and white. Yet still, a visit to the Willamette Valley in the fall before and during harvest time is one of the agricultural landscape's most unique and striking sights.

The photographs are organized in a sequence that begins with the hop plant and an overview of hopyards, followed by establishing a hopyard's unique landscape of poles, wires, strings, and the subsequent maintenance during the growing cycle. Photographs of the hop harvest follow, emphasizing the pickers, representative of the thousands of individuals who worked over several generations picking, baling, hauling, and drying. Life in camps is documented as well. The final images are celebratory, showing workers around and atop the hop dryers. The photographs in each of these stages are organized chronologically. The bulk of the photographs are from the era that predated mechanical picking that dominates after 1950, with only a few images depicting contemporary practice.

CAPTIONS

The captions for each image contain the title and location (if known) and descriptive information as it is found in the archive. Also noted are the archival source and photographer (if known). In addition, reflecting the diverse content of photographic images, the text contains a wide range of information. Collectively it illuminates the cultural landscape of the hopscape. Most common are first-person accounts drawn from oral histories, most of which were recorded in 1982 by the Benton County Historical Society and the Lane County Historical Museum. Where possible these stories refer to the accompanying photograph in terms of the location or activity. However, many do not and are intended to generally reveal the experience of those who worked in hopyards. It was these workers, along with the growers and their more permanent workers, who made possible this landscape. Some text describes individual growers and organizations, as well the processes and materials that are the hop landscapes. Where possible, individuals or groups of individuals are identified. There are also copies of advertisements seeking pickers as they appeared in Oregon newspapers.

SOURCES

The photographs in this collection were assembled from archives in western Oregon, the historical region of hop growing. The archives at the Oregon Hops and Brewers Archive at Oregon State University and the Oregon Historical Society in Portland, which have collected material from throughout the state, are exceptional. Photos were also collected from the historical societies in Lane, Josephine, and Polk Counties, the Independence Historical Museum, Oregon State Library, University of Oregon, Library of Congress, and Thomas Robinson, as well as individual photographers and on-line collections. The photographs in these archives were assembled from donations from hop growers and their associations, photographer archives, as well as individual donations. The images in the book were chosen from thousands of examples based on their quality as photographs and those best able to tell the historic story of the hopscape.

Hop cones varieties, 1930

SOURCE: OHBA, OSU Special Collections and Archives Research Center, Corvallis, Oregon, Agricultural Experiment Station Records, 1889–2002 (RG 025)

Hops are a dioecious perennial with male and female plants. The female hop cone is harvested. Within the female flowers are yellow grains called lupulin. This complex substance is the flavoring agent of the hop, offering both taste and odor. Hops are categorized as either a flavor or aroma type or a bitter, also known as alpha type. The alpha acid in the hop is the main bittering agent, while other oils in the hop contribute to the flavor. There are many hop varieties, with aromas as varied as grass, grapefruit, chocolate, pepper, mint, apricot, and tangerine. Different beers are characterized by the different hop varieties, with aromas ranging from subtle to powerful and alpha type ranging from modestly to strongly bitter. Hops also have antiseptic properties and act as a preservative, improving the stability of the beverage. While the viticulture term *terroir* is not applied to hops, local conditions do determine acidity, which contributes to the level of bitterness.

Three main hop varieties were planted in 1933: Late Cluster, Early Cluster (a variety that originated in a mutation from a yard of Late Cluster near Albany), and Fuggles, more resistant to downy mildew, which began its spread in 1929. Many of the new varieties developed over the years have been the product of research at Oregon State University. These included Cascade, officially released in 1971, as well as Nugget and Willamette, two varieties that now account for two-thirds of all hops grown in Oregon. Growers continue to experiment with new varieties. Hop varieties grown in Oregon as of 2018 include Cascade, Centennial, Chinook, Citra, Crystal, Fuggle, Golding, Magnum, Mosaic, Mt. Hood, Nugget, Perle, Simcoe, Styerling, Super Galena, Tettnanger, and Willamette.

Hops are no longer graded, but a century ago hops were classified as fancy, choice, prime, medium, or poor. They were graded by their size, brightness in color, flavor, odor, health, and quantity of lupulin. (Myrick 1909)

19

Man with spike on cluster, 1932

SOURCE: OHBA, OSU Special Collections and Archives Research Center, Corvallis, Oregon, Agricultural Experiment Station Records, 1889–2002 (RG 025)

Since the 1930s Oregon State University in Corvallis, in cooperation with the US Department of Agriculture, has been the leading center for hop breeding and research in the United States. As Oregon's land-grant institution, OSU is dedicated to an agricultural mission. From 1965 until 1999, OSU/USDA hop breeder Dr. Al Haunold pioneered the development of twenty varieties, most notably the aptly named Cascade, which—with its aroma and resistance to downy mildew—became the cornerstone variety of the craft brewing industry as it developed in the 1980s.

The comments from Herman Goschie, a second-generation hop grower, are a testament to the continuing practice and innovation of hop growers.

> We grow about 30 percent of the old what they call Fuggle variety, which is an English flavor-type variety. Then probably 40 or 45 percent, 50 percent I guess of another English variety, it's called a Bullion, or Brewer's Gold. . . . We also have a few of a new variety that was developed down there called Columbia. Then we have some experimental (they're experimental to us, but they're old European varieties from the continent) and one is called Styrian. This comes from Yugoslavia. We have a Tettnang which comes from an area in Germany near the Swiss border, and we have a Herschbruck which is a relatively new German variety. I guess that's all we're growing now.
>
> —1982 interview with Herman Goschie

Clearing a field for hops

SOURCE: Independence Heritage Museum

Trees have been felled and stumps are being uprooted in this photograph.

James Seavey Hopyard, Springfield, 1914

PHOTOGRAPHER: Smith Montjoy. SOURCE: Courtesy of the Lane County Historical Museum

In this photo, pickers are at work, harvesting hops on a horse-drawn wagon.

But the first hops, first picking, instead of the pickers calling out "wire down," and "sacks full" or something, he hollered "hop pole." They pulled the pole out of the ground and they cut the vine right off at the ground, with, well, they had a kind of a hooked knife on a stick with a handle about so long. Just cut that off right at the top of the ground, pulled the pole out and they picked hops in a cot. It was generally a pair of mules about five feet apart and there was a bolted thing and you'd close the darned thing up and carry it along when it wasn't full of hops. When it was full of hops, about 50 pounds. If you didn't get somebody to help you sack it up right away, well, you mashed them down, I've seen 120 pounds in one of those crazy things and they couldn't hardly drag it along anymore. But they put a pole across between those mules ears, they called them, and pull this pole out of the ground, cut the vine off right at the ground and lay it right up against it. Well, when the hops were all picked, the vines were cut off and the poles, they were all down on the ground. Well, then we'd gather up those vines and burn them and put the poles in this hop drier where the furnaces were. Then, during winter if there was any of them broke, they'd repair those and get them ready for another year. The wire and string and stuff didn't come into it until later, after that. But I never pulled poles.
   —1982 interview with Charles Staley (born 1891, near Verbort)

Hopyard, 1880

PHOTOGRAPHER: Angelus Studio. SOURCE: PHO37_b004_AG001760. Or. Digital df71p436

"Hoppicking Time is Holiday in Oregon

"Hop picking time is the gayest, most carefree, easy money time in all the year.

"Poets and story writers have from time immemorial lauded the beauty of the hop fields and flung about them aromatic interest. They deserve all the superlatives in the market, for the crop is one of the most beautiful grown. The long vines are festooned from post to post and crowned with clusters of bell-like blossoms, marvelously delicate as to its shadings and wafting as gentle fragrance, grateful to the olfactory sense. The running vines completely embower the slackened wire from which hang pendant myriads of tips and tendrils that wave and beckon in the breezes that sweep across the mountain tops. They appear to be millions of welcoming hands bidding one to come in and join the fun. Beyond the hop fields are the yellow fields of ripened grain and in the midst winds the beautiful Willamette River, bordered with fir and alder, oak and maple, while on either side of the valley rise the mountains, the Coast Range on the west, and in the east, softly veiled by a purple haze, the snowcapped Cascades."

　　—*Sunday Oregonian,* September 24, 1911

Hop field with donkey, circa 1880

PHOTOGRAPHER: Angelus Studio. SOURCE: PH037_b001_AG00020 or or.digital – d71f

Angelus Studio was a professional photographic studio in Portland. Early photographers included George Weister (1862–1922) and Arthur Prentiss. The Angelus Commercial Photo Company, established around 1911, specialized in commercial subjects. "We photograph Construction Work, Interiors and Exteriors of Buildings, Real Estate Views, Machinery, Furniture, Automobiles, Catalog Work, etc." The studio acquired all of Weister and Prentiss's early negatives, including their photographs of hop fields.

Hop rows, 1880

PHOTOGRAPHER: Angelus Studio. SOURCE: Or. Digital Archive d71fj17. Pho37_b001_600029

Encountering the Crosby Hop Farm for the first time, Zak Schroerlucke described the experience as "seeing a celebrity for the first time," noting the "magic and wonderment of it—shady, cool, quiet, magical." Working in the hopyard, Bradley Barnette enjoys the "multi-sensory sights, smells, and sounds." As the hops mature, agronomist Ann Iskra finds the hopyard from July through fall harvest as "impressive and peaceful. When the hops are fully grown, the tall bines feel forest-like and can block out the world, making you feel like you are away from the pace of your normal life."

    —From an April 30, 2019, interview with the author at the Crosby Hop barn in Woodburn

31

Hop poles, pre-trellis system, 1880

PHOTOGRAPHER: Angelus Photo. SOURCE: PH037_b00003 Angelus. Or. Digital – df71fj04

"The Krebs began the hauling and distributing of trellis poles for their big yard this week. It will require 9,000 poles and all have been cut on the Krebs place. None are less than five inches in diameter and they will be 17 feet high allowing for resetting. The trellis wire will be 11 feet from the ground. The end of the poles will be dipped in carbolineum avenarius, a preservative."

    —*West Side Enterprise*, Independence, July 21, 1904

Bill Swanson hopyard, Grants Pass, circa 1900

SOURCE: Josephine County Historical Society

One of Oregon's famous hopyards, circa 1900

PHOTOGRAPHER: Brooks Photo. SOURCE: Polk County Historical Society

OF OREGON'S FAMOUS HOP YARDS.
BROOKS PHOTO.

Matthews Hop Yard, Lane County, circa 1900

SOURCE: Courtesy of the Lane County Historical Museum, gn7265

In this photograph, note the hopyard, pickers, sacks on horse-drawn wagon, and driers, and the presence of men, women, children, and babies.

"Wire down!" It's a call I remember from hop field days in the 30s when I was just tall enough to see over the bog basket and "Mom help pick." Those were the summers when J. W. Seavey had acres and acres of those climbing vines on high wires along the bottom land of the Mohawk River not far from Armitage Bridge.

How can I tell the younger generation about what hop picking was like—before those memories disappear? Well, I remember mostly the feel and the smell of the hops, and the interminable time it took to fill that huge basket. Lots of fun and teasing went on in the yard and I remember being hoisted into a basket, dropped among all that fragrance, where I'd feel a scratchy sort of fluffiness all around me, and if I didn't get lifted out again "righty now!" I'd thrash around and tip the basket over, which was not the desirable thing to do—dirty hops were as bad as too many leaves.

After a diversion like that I'd pick "like a little girl" for a while, stripping hops off those long streamers into the containers, and oh! The feel of that. Without gloves or taped fingers, hands would soon be sore because the hops were really rough and prickly, not soft and fluffy at all.

The big moment, which seemed to come too seldom, was when the basket was judged full enough to be dumped. Then it got emptied into the biggest, longest, widest sack any child ever romped in. If I crawled inside an empty one, I could see the light through the loosely woven burlap. Inside there, the smell sur- rounded one, a smell of many hops long since dumped in the old hop drier. The long sacks were used over and over and they soon captured the pungent aroma of the blossoms. That scent was hard to define—a sort of musty emanation that was most noticeable when the blossoms were bruised—like a hundred mugs of beer I'd say today, for such the hops were used. But in those days I just knew it was a strong smell, not unpleasant. The smell would get all over your work clothes and body, and would stay there . . .

—1982 interview with M. E. Culver, Lane County Historical Museum

Panorama of the Zoller Hopyard, Mission Bottom, Salem, 1913, with seven hundred hops under cultivation

SOURCE: Zoller Hop Company Records (MSS Zoller), OSU Special Collections and Archives Research Center, Corvallis, Oregon; Bush House Museum, Salem Art Association, Photo ID number bhp0288

Headquartered in New York City, the Zoller family owned a brewery supply business and were pioneers of the brewing industry. Charles Zoller was born in Germany in 1852 and emigrated in 1872; his father-in-law Christian Schmidt was a successful Philadelphia brewer. In 1906, Charles and his son, Christian, purchased a farm from Henry Ottenheimer of Independence and established the Zoller Hop Company with D. P. MacCarthy as manager. MacCarthy, from South Africa, was educated in England and came to Oregon at age twenty-one in 1894. Ultimately the Zollers became successful brokers for the sale of Willamette Valley hops nationally. In 1918 MacCarthy purchased the Zoller Company and the name was changed to D. P. MacCarthy & Son.

41

Hoeing, 1931

SOURCE: OHBA, OSU Special Collections and Archives Research Center, Corvallis, Oregon, Agricultural Experiment Station Records, 1889–2002 (RG 025). Identifier RG25_1931 hoeing, p. 46

In *The Hop*, Herbert Myrick reports how Oregon hop grower A. J. Wolcott summarizes his practice in Oregon:

"Cultivation consists first of plowing the yard early in the spring with two horses and a turning plow, throwing the dirt away from the hill, then level down with either a cultivator or harrow and then cross plow the same and level down again. After this, the yard should be done every two or three weeks with either a good cultivator or heavy disk harrow until about June 20, when all cultivation should cease as cultivation after that date destroys the small feeders from the roots, which commence top shoot out near the surface and fill the space between hills. Destroying these will cause the hops to take another start and make them late in ripening. After all the cultivation is done, the ground should be gone over each way with a clod masher or smoother, made the right width to go between the rows without damaging the vines. This levels and firms the soil and prevents evaporation during the long dry spell of July and August. The hop hills should be hoed as often as necessary to keep down the weeds, and if none is permitted to go to seed for a few weeks, this will become very small task."

—Herbert Myrick, *The Hop* (Springfield, MA: Orange Judd Company, 1909)

Stringing wire to poles on horse-drawn wagon, 1938

PHOTOGRAPHER: Ben Maxwell. SOURCE: Oregon Historical Society, Folder Ag-Hops Wkrs., Neg. 11948

"Cedar was preferred in the bottom-land yards where the growth of hop is usually abundant and requires a high, sturdy trellis. Fir is usually cheaper initial cost and has been reasonably satisfactory on the valley-floor yards where lower trellises are satisfactory for the vine growth obtained there."
—*Cost and Efficiency in Producing Hops in Oregon*,
Agricultural Station Bulletin, 1939

In 1902, poles cost two cents in Oregon. In 2019 four-to-five-inch by twenty-one-foot poles were twenty-nine dollars. End poles cost thirty-eight to eighty dollars depending on their diameter.

Ben Maxwell, the photographer, was a Salem journalist, historian, and photographer. From 1939 to 1965 he had a daily column, "Nuggets," in the *Capital Journal*. He took his own photographs as well as amassing a collection of historical images. Photographic supplies were expensive so to cut costs he became known as "One-Shot Maxwell." His archive is found in the collection of the Salem Public Library.

Securing wire to poles with tractor pulling high tower, 1952

SOURCE: OHBA, OSU Special Collections and Archives Research Center, Corvallis, Oregon, Gifford Photographic Collection, circa 1885–1958 (P 218). Identifier P218 SG 4 0849

HOP POLES.

Parties wishing to purchase cedar hop poles or fence posts can have the same delivered aboard the Oregon Pacific cars at Berry, Marion Co., Or., in quantities and prices to suit. For further particulars call on or write to

J. L. BERRY,

.50   Berry, Oregon.

SOURCE: *The Independence West Sider,* April 27, 1894

SOURCE: Oregon Historical Society, Folder Ag-Hops Wrks., Neg. ORFH181630

By that time we had a high sled, and my sister and I used to train on there, and we used to play games and sing songs and everything as we drove along. We had this old horse, and she would pull this high sled while we trained. When we wanted her to go, we told her to "Go" and when she would stop, we told her "Whoa." She was trained well enough to go around this and skip one row and go into the next one. But my father was on the sled one day and she turned a little too short and hit a post and he whipped her for it and she would never try it again. We had to pry her from then on. Then they decided they would put higher wires and then they put two strings and split them and that gave them more air.

Interviewer: How many vines per string?

We put out three to start with, or when we only just had one string and one wire, we put three vines up. Those hills all had to be trimmed and suckered. But I never worked in the hops after I was married. My husband didn't believe in that. He didn't think that I should go out.

—1982 interview with Rosa Cole (born 1891, Silverton)

SOURCE: Oregon Historical Society, File 20-1, aghopsIMG

"In Oregon those who adopt the pole system use young firs, which grow abundantly in the state. They aim to get a pole three inches thick and about sixteen feet long. . . . Stand the poles upright in a tank containing two feet of creosote or coal tar, and let them simmer over a slow fire for the night; this will prevent the butts from rotting and is a big saving."
    —Herbert Myrick, *The Hop* (Springfield, MA: Orange Judd Company, 1909)

"On the Pacific coast, when a crop is picked the first year, poles are set before the roots are planted, which prevents injury or disturbing the roots afterward. With a long dibble having a steel sharpened point, a hole is made, about eighteen inches deep, into which the pole is stuck and left vertical. A man can set about 600 poles in a day. A short stake is set the tenth hill in every tenth row to indicate when a male root is planted."
    —Herbert Myrick, *The Hop* (Springfield, MA: Orange Judd Company, 1909)

Women stringers

SOURCE: Independence Heritage Museum, 2003014015

Beth Monroe, born on the hop farm that her father managed, described life on Livesley Hop, later called Roberts.

Well, I worked on the hop ranch from the time I was able to do any outside work at all. When school was out, we started with the training of the hops from the time that they came up out of the ground—you have to train them around the strings that take them to the wire. Then my younger brother and I, when we were quite young, rode the sleds. Have you ever seen a hop sled? They were drawn by horses, one horse per sled. They were probably six feet high. We climbed up a ladder on the back. They went down between two rows and you would train the hops. Now hops grow a certain way, and you had to train them on the wires. This was when the wires were lower than they were eventually when they used hop pickers. But we had to train them on the wire to keep them from falling down, and they held themselves up there. These wires were on a trellis so that they could be let down so people could pick the hops.

—1982 interview with Beth Monroe (born Livesley Hop, Salem)

Stringers, James Seavey Hopyard, 1914

PHOTOGRAPHER: Smith Montjoy. SOURCE: Courtesy of the Lane County Historical Museum, SM 206

At James Seavey's hopyard on the McKenzie River north of Springfield, twine is hung around the stringers' necks like scarves.

The photo is by Smith Montjoy, an amateur photographer who documented the area in and around Springfield. He worked at the Booth-Kelly Mill, the city's largest employer, for forty-two years. He started taking pictures in 1910 and made most of his photographs in the subsequent decade. He was known for always carrying his bellows camera on his motorcycle, an Indian brand originally produced from 1901 to 1953 in another Springfield, in Massachusetts. His photographs are in the collection of the Springfield Museum.

Japanese workers tying strings, Wigrich Ranch, 1930

SOURCE: Independence Heritage Museum

In a field near Independence, a 1912 article stated, "50 Japanese pickers were at work, congregating in groups along each vine line, while native pickers preferred to have a row devoted to one person exclusively. . . . Among the pickers in the various yards every grade of society was to be represented. It was obvious that the oldest profession was well represented by former members. . . . Yet almost side by side, there were Portland high school girls, intent on working for a little pocket money for school, not to speak of getting one of the finest vacations in Oregon at the same time. . . . One could make distinctions between those who were considered amateur pickers versus professionals. When it got too sunny or hot, many worked just in the morning and took the afternoon off." (*Sunday Oregonian*, September 29, 1912, p. 18)

Woman stringer, 1938

PHOTOGRAPHER: Ben Maxwell. SOURCE: Oregon Historical Society

The "strings" that support the bines are natural fibers. The most popular twine is made of coir. The word "coir" is derived from the Malaysian word *kayar*, meaning cord. Coir is a coconut fiber and is made from the long husk fibers that are harvested between the inner and outer hard shell of the coconut. The husks are soaked in brackish water for six to ten months. The fiber is then easily removed, beaten, and dried. The fibers are sun dried and then twisted together by hand or machine to make roped strands five to six meters in length, which are affixed to the trellis wire. Coir is a strong, malleable fiber that is rot resistant and lasts the growing season. Coir is now imported from Sri Lanka and India, which produce 90 percent of the world's supply. Coir yarn comes in bales twenty feet, six inches in length that weigh roughly four hundred to six hundred pounds, depending on their moisture content. After the harvest the strings are composted.

Wire stringing and staking, 1938

SOURCE: Oregon Historical Society, Folder Ag-Hops Wkrs.

Strings are fastened into the ground during twining. A hop clip applicator has a handle and a foot pad to push the string into the ground and then fasten it with a W clip, so called because of its shape. The clips come five thousand to a box.

Stringing wires at Eola Yard, Polk County, 1941

SOURCE: OHBA, OSU Special Collections and Archives Research Center, Corvallis, Oregon, Harriet's Photograph Collection, 1868–1996 (P HC). Identifier HC0972

A string is attached to wires for each hill of hops. Twine is also used in stringing. It comes in twenty-two-foot lengths with ten thousand strings to a box. They arrive on a pallet with forty-four hanks per pallet (a hank is the coiled unit of a yarn or twine); each hank has three hundred strings. The bottom three feet of the strings are treated with a solution to counter rot.

Armenians training the hops, Arslanian Brothers Contracting Company, 1930

SOURCE: Independence Heritage Museum, IMG6264

The way we trained hops, of course, when we trained them from the ground up, well we trained them by hand. Just stand on the ground and twist the vines around the strings and let them grow on up. And after they got on up to the wires and trained on the wires, why we had great big high buggies, regular buggies, and one horse on it and a platform up on top. We would reach on both sides and go right down the middle of the row, see. Just wide enough to go through. You'd train the hop vines on the wires.

　　—1982 interview with Tom Kraemer (born 1918, Mt. Angel)

Women stringing a hop field, circa 1980

SOURCE: Oregon Hop Growers Association Records, 1912–2011 (MSS OHGA), OSU Special Collections and Archives Research Center, Corvallis, Oregon. Identifier MSS OHGA 208

Hops grow along the ground until they encounter an object they can climb. The growing hop plant must be supported. Growers train the bines to grow vertically to maximize the production of the hop cone.

Stringing trellis on platform drawn by tractor, 1985

SOURCE: Oregon Hop Growers Association Records, 1912–2011 (MSS OHGA), OSU Special Collections and Archives Research Center, Corvallis, Oregon. Identifier MSS OHGA 178

Spraying, experimental red spider control, 1940, at Pankalla Hop Ranch, Corvallis

SOURCE: OHBA, OSU Special Collections and Archives Research Center, Corvallis, Oregon, Agricultural Experiment Station Records, 1889–2002 (RG 025). Originally published in "Hop Pests and Their Control: A Report of the Control of the Hop Red Spider and Other Closely Related Problems During the Season of 1940," by H. E. Morrison and J. D. (Jack) Vertrees.

Rosa Cole described spraying for red spiders, which could hardly be seen with the naked eye, around 1910:

> They had a large iron kettle and they built a fire. They hung this kettle over the fire and they boiled these Quasha chips and whale oil soap. This was a very thick emulsion, when they had it done. They would put so many pounds or bucketsful in this barrel of water on the sled and thin it down. I don't know how they measured it exactly. I guess I never paid too much attention how much they put in there. But I know that that's how they made their spray.

When interviewed sixty years later, Carl Ehlen told of spraying with two other boys around 1920:

> We sprayed hops for aphids—the spray tank was on a four-wheel wagon pulled by a Fordson tractor. The spray solution was a water-whale oil soap—nicotine—a gasoline engine and spray pump as on top of sprayer. Two of us walked behind the sprayer—each of us carried a spray nozzle and hose attached to pump. Each of us spraying a row of hops and we walked—we had no protection for our eyes, nose, or face. We were soaked with spray. One night when I got home I became very sick to my stomach and threw up. All that came up was dark liquid. I went to bed unable to eat and do not remember if I help spraying hops any more times.

Irrigating hops, 1914

PHOTOGRAPHER: Smith Montjoy. SOURCE: Courtesy of the Lane County Historical Museum, SM228

Hops need sufficient water during their growing season, but with irrigation they can grow in a wide variety of soil conditions. While there are 150 days of rain per year in the Willamette Valley, with an average of forty to forty-five inches of rain, summers are very dry with almost no rain. Irrigation in the Willamette Valley commences when the rains stop and as twining of the bines begins. Most contemporary hopyards employ drip irrigation systems.

In this photo, three young men dig an irrigation ditch at James Seavey's hopyard. Note the hop bines climbing over the cracked bare soil.

Hop pickers arriving at Independence, Oregon, circa 1910

SOURCE: Independence Heritage Museum

"For the past ten days they have been pouring in by team and train. All last week along the principal roads centering in Independence were almost continuous processions of teams bearing hop pickers afield and clouds of dust enveloped the much-travelled highways. All last week trains ran behind time because of the unusual number of hop pickers and hop pickers' baggage and at many times there was congestion of traffic on Independence streets and at the ferry landing. As many as sixty-five teams have been counted at one time between Padock's store and Wilson's grocery, a space of scarcely a block. On Friday, after waiting for the hop pickers to alight and transfer of their baggage, the afternoon trains pulled out an hour late. There were three cars jammed to the ceiling with baggage and though the entire train crew and stations force worked like Trojans in transferring it to the station, the trains were delayed until the middle of the afternoon.

"On the same day 120 teams and 600 pickers were transferred across the ferry landing, at times being blocked for rods with teams and people waiting their turn. The streets likewise were blocked at times, so that one must wend his way by tortuous course to pass between the teams.

"The arrival of hop pickers at Independence, the disbursing point, is one that will hold place in memory of those here this year. Though dust be-grimed and weary from long travel, they are disposed to cheerfulness and are best on making the most of their hop-picking outing. Most are now domiciled in their hop-picking homes. The picture has changed, the pilgrimage has ended."

—*West Side Enterprise*, Independence, Oregon, September 6, 1904

Hop pickers ariving at
Independence Ore,

"Rush to get seats on hay wagon for hop fields. Hop ranchers are anxious to get the pickers as they are to get a job."

SOURCE: Oregon Historical Society, Folder Ag-Hops Wkrs.

Note the women are not yet dressed for work in the hopyards and their suitcases are packed for the coming weeks.

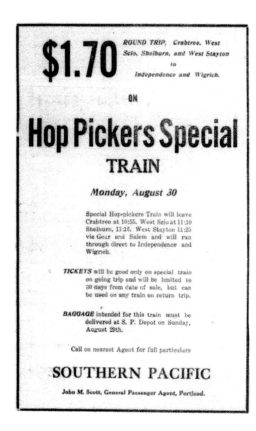

SOURCE: *Stayton Mail*, August 26, 1915

YWCA tent, 1880

PHOTOGRAPHER: Angelus Studio. SOURCE: Or. Digital df71fp39r

In an article lauding the "Pure Democracy" found in the labor of the hop fields, the *Oregonian* praised the efforts of the YWCA:

> "The Association has established itself in a great tent, jocularly called in the field the tabernacle. The women are earnestly striving to make the tent attractive and to set up friendly relations with the pickers. They desire to lighten the labors, increase the comforts and lessen the temptations of young women in the hopfields. . . . The majority go with their families. But, there are scores of unprotected girls, who have no one to care for their comfort or advise them in times of stress. To such the Association would extend the warm hand of friendship."
> —*Sunday Oregonian,* September 29, 1907

Native American pickers from the Warm Springs Reservation at the Templeton Hopyard, Linn County, 1884. Note their arrival at the yard in full regalia.

PHOTOGRAPHER: Joseph Holt Templeton. SOURCE: Oregon Historical Society, Box Lot 603, box 22MG E613b or OHS orh24370

Ezra Meeker notes that Indians came to the Northwest for what they called "hops time" and that they were the primary laborers. They were from tribes in Puget Sound but also British Columbia and even Alaska. They came as much as three hundred miles by canoe, "bringing with them their dogs and their cats, their chickens and their trumpery as though they had come to stay all summer." He wrote that "They were of all conditions, the old and young, the blind and maimed, the workers and the idlers, making a motley mess curious to look upon." Yet he described them as "inveterate and reliable workers, going to the hop field as soon as they can see, carrying their dinners with them and remaining until pitch dark." (Ezra Meeker, *Hop Culture in the United States*, 1883)

Pickers, Clutes yard, Applegate, Josephine County, 1899 or 1900

SOURCE: Josephine County Historical Society

The box of Peruna The Great Tonic in the foreground was a "medicine" concocted by a Pennsylvania physician, Dr. Samuel Hartman, in the 1880s and marketed as a cure for catarrh. Hartman's advertising claimed that "pneumonia was catarrh of the lungs, so was tuberculosis. Cancer sores were catarrh of the mouth; appendicitis, catarrh of the appendix; chronic indigestion, catarrh of the stomach; mumps, catarrh of the glands; Bright's disease, catarrh of the kidneys, even yellow fever, another form of ca-tarrh." In fact, Peruna was 28 percent alcohol (later dropped to 18 percent) and water, with a flavor cube and burned sugar for color. In 1905 the Department of the Interior forbade the sale of Peruna to Indians. Given its high alcohol content, Peruna was particularly popular during Prohibition. Despite evidence that Peruna was a quack medicine, it was sold until the 1940s.

Oregon hops farms were part of larger corporate enterprises. Founded by John I. Haas, the Barth-Haas Group is the country's largest hop grower. Now headquartered in the Yakima Valley, Barth-Haas previously had major hopyards near Grants Pass. John Curry, who managed one of these yards, said, "Hops from Josephine County may go anywhere on the globe now. John I. Haas sells hops to almost all breweries in the world."

Charles Lathrop's Grants Pass hopyard was established in 1936. His final harvest was in 1989. Only in recent years has hop growing returned to the Rogue Valley.

CLUTES Yard
APPLEGATE HOP PICKING

1899
OR
1900

Pickers, Oregon City, circa 1890

SOURCE: Oregon Historical Society, Folder Ag-Hops Wkrs.

Rosa Cole, who began working when she was fourteen, describes stringing and the switch from pole to trellis hops around 1906:

> I started working in the hop yard, tying strings. By this time, they had put in wires and tied the strings top and bottom. They cut the strings the right length and we put them around our necks and crossed them here and put them around and tied them in the back (around the waist). Then we took ahold of the string here and tied it on the wire and walked away and it just pulled out. All along. Then the wires were raised up and we pulled them down and tied them at the bottom. . . .
>
> These pole hops, they had to cut those little poles and they only was as high as this house, maybe nine feet or so. You can see what the hops are now. A mile up there. It gives the hops more room to spread out and have more air and sunlight. Cause when they just went up this little pole, why then they just all hung down this one pole. Then they put the wires and they had one wire.

Preston Berry's pickers, Fox Valley, east of Lyons, Marion County, 1889

Hop Pickers' Supplies

For Men, Women and Children

Everything necessary for the hop fields will be found here at prices that will pay you to completely outfit yourselves at a saving.

MEXICAN SUN HATS
wide brims, all sizes for women and children, regular 25c kind, each
15 Cents

DRESS CALICOES
100 pieces Light and Dark Calico,
6 Cents Yard

MEN'S SOX
60 dozen Men's Heavy Work Sox
5 Cents Pair

WORK GLOVES
For Hop Pickers. Heavy Canvas kind, all sizes.
3 Pairs for 25 Cents

WOMEN'S STOCKINGS
Plain Ribbed Tops, Double Soles.
12 1-2 Cents Per Pair

COTTON BLANKETS
Full size, either white, grey or tan, with colored borders.
50c, 75c and $1.00

COMFORTERS
50 well made comforters, best white cotton filled, a good value at $2.
Special, $1.50

COTTON TOWELS
50 doz hemmed cotton towels good size.
5 Cents Each

Ladies' Percalo Wrappers
85c, $1.00, $1.25

J. M. Nolan & Son
QUALITY STORE

Coat Sweaters
$1.50, $2.50, $3.50

SOURCE: *Daily Times Gazette*
(Corvallis), August 28, 1909

87

Pickers, Wigrich Ranch, 1929

SOURCE: Independence Heritage Museum

SOURCE: *Independence West Sider,*
July 21, 1893

No. 1
1929

Postcard, 1910

SOURCE: OHBA , OSU Special Collections and Archives Research Center, Corvallis, Oregon, Brewing and Fermentation Research Collection. Identifier OHBC_unknown_postcard

Postcards of hopyards and pickers date from the first decade of the twentieth century. Beginning in 1907 the US Post Office allowed private citizens to write on the backs of postcards. In 1908 seven hundred million postcards were mailed in the United States and postcard collecting became a common hobby. German printers provided most of the printing, but this ended with World War I; thereafter, American printers dominated. Writing and sending a postcard, which cost less than a letter (postcard postage was one penny until 1952) and required less writing, was a way to keep in touch, and a personal gesture of sharing an experience, especially of where one had travelled, even if it was close to home. "Wish you were here" may have been the most common sentiment.

Postcards offered scenes of American life: cities from Main Street to downtown, transportation of every kind of vehicle, scenic areas, landmarks, monuments, libraries, churches, hotels, parks, courthouses, even humorous events. There were postcards of industry and the agricultural occupations and landscapes: miners, fishermen, loggers, and ranchers. Images of hop pickers that showed the work in the landscape offered an image of both a place and the activity.

162 – Hop Picking.

Pickers, Grants Pass, John Ranzau Hopyard

SOURCE: Josephine County Historical Society

This poem by Mrs. F. E. Turner, a hop grower's wife from Independence, appeared in
The Hopper in December 1948, in answer to a previously published poem, "The Hop Picker's
Lament." It is a fine summary of the work that precedes the work of the pickers.

The Hop Grower's Reply

Of the October Hopper, a bit of time I've
    Spent.
I wonder if the picker, the inside woes
    could know
Of the poor old lonely duffer, who has to
    make hops grow?
From March until September he's up at
    break of day
To tackle all the problems that makes his
    hair turn gray.
He goes out to the hop yard to twine, to
    plow to train.
Wondering whether tomorrow will bring
    Sun—or rain.
Praying between his cussing that the hops
    will be O.K.,

So that you, the real "hop picker" again
    will make your way.
Back to the Oregon Hop yards to harvest
    the same old hops
He's saving from lice and mildew that
    threaten to take the crops.
The early hours you complain of we keep
    the whole long year.
And when it's time for dusting both day
    and night we hear
Those awful machines in action, a noise
    we can hardly bear.
Till all the folks in earshot are ready to
    tear their hair.
When you pick the hops, remember, if
    you think the pay is small.

It's sure, but the grower never knows if
    there'll be any market at all
He may be working for nothing, working
    and worrying too.
Planning for next year's problems before
    this year's are through
Hops are a gamble from first to last—but
    let's see you back next year.
And nothing preventing, we'll be on hand
    to greet you with right good cheer.
So here is a toast to the picker, and here's
    to the grower as well.
May we meet next year in the same old
    yard.
We'll be there as—well, well—guess
    that's about enough.

Pickers on the Wigrich Ranch, including Chinese workers, 1899

SOURCE: Independence Heritage Museum, Wigrich 010

Chinese settlers in the nineteenth century were predominantly men laboring in mining and railroad construction. Oregon's Chinese population grew from 3,330 in 1870 to 10,397 in 1900. In the Willamette Valley, Chinese laborers worked in commercial agriculture, lumbering, fisheries, and canneries as well as domestic service. The bulk of the Chinese community lived in the Chinatown area of Portland. Article IX, Section 8 of the Oregon Constitution (1857) stated that "No Chinaman, not a resident of the state at the adoption of this constitution, shall ever hold any real estate or mining claim, or work any mining claim therein." There were periodic conflicts and even expulsions of Chinese from communities. In 1882, Congress passed the first federal Chinese Exclusion Act, which specifically banned the entry of Chinese laborers to the United States and was not repealed until 1943. Despite these laws, a few Chinese leased land in the valley. In spite of legal restrictions and persistent racial bias, Chinese and Japanese persons, like other Portland residents, joined the hop harvest.

Holland Hopyard, near the town of Crow, Lane County, 1904

PHOTOGRAPHER: Henry R. Ross. SOURCE: Courtesy of the Lane County Historical Museum, gn4671

George Leasure purchased rootstock from Adam Weisner, who had the first hopyard in the valley, and established a five-acre hopyard in the bottomland outside of Eugene. It was the first hopyard in Oregon to yield a harvest, and an 1899 *Eugene City Guard* article noted that it was still producing three thousand pounds per acre. The article also noted that annual flooding of the banks of the Willamette was gradually eating away at the hopyards.

Pickers with wire down and man on pole, 1908

SOURCE: OHBC 1908 Postcard published by Drake Bros., Silverton, OR. Oregon Historical Society, Folder Ag-Hops Wkrs.

"The field, filled with pickers, was an interesting sight. In one row a man and his wife picked together while small children crawled around in the dirt at their feet; over a little was a woman with six offspring picking in her basket; just beyond was a giddy girl with a forward boy she had met on the train—both picking away and passing cheap compliments; away to the right was red-cheeked German girl crying because her clumsy fingers made work slow; near her were two bright high school girls eager to earn money for clothes; not far away was a widow of nearly fifty with her aged mother, making small headway with the hops; I taught her what I had learned and then things went better."
—*Maclean Magazine*, Summer 1907

Pickers, Livesley hopyard

SOURCE: Oregon Historical Society, Folder Ag-Hops Wkrs.

Thomas Livesley grew up in Wisconsin, the son of a hop farmer. Moving to Oregon in 1894, he continued the family tradition by founding the T. A. Livesley Co. By 1915, he owned four hop ranches near Salem that produced one tenth of all Oregon hops, and one thirtieth of all hops produced worldwide. He became known as the "Hop King of Oregon," a more modest claim than Washington hop farmer Ezra Meeker, author of the 1880 book *Hop Culture in the United States,* who declared himself "Hop King of the World." Livesley also owned extensive hop fields in Canada. He went on to be elected mayor of Salem and to the Oregon House of Representatives. Successful as a farmer, politician, and banker, he built a mansion in Salem in 1922 designed by Ellis F. Lawrence, founder of the University of Oregon School of Architecture. In 1988 the house was donated to the State of Oregon as the official residence of the governor and renamed Mahonia Hall after the state flower (*Mahonia aquifolium*).

On September 25, 1914, the *Independence Monitor* reported that visitors, including "two moving picture men," toured Livesley's ranch. Livesley bragged about his production of seven hundred to twelve hundred pounds of cured hops, his nursery for hop roots, and especially an underground piping system that allowed spraying from standpipes and now was getting three thousand pounds an acre. He noted: "Growing hops is not a haphazard proposition. Science wins the game as elsewhere." Livesley also praised his new hop-picking machine that would replace the pickers. This was premature, for machine did not come into common use until the early 1950s.

Pickers with hats

SOURCE: Oregon Historical Society, Folder Ag-Hops Wkrs.

Bessie G. Murphy, who began picking at age twelve and continued into her twenties, describes her experience:

> At the time I picked hops with my mother and younger brother, we got up fairly early in the morning in order to have time to help with so-called chores on a farm; prepare to eat breakfast; and pack lunch to take to the hop yard. My father fed and harnessed and hitched up the horse and buggy—all ready to go the approximately four-mile journey to the hop yard. He stayed home and ran the farm as usual. That time of the year was plowing and planting time. . . . My father did not approve of my mother working in the hop-yard; it was too hard on her to work the long hours necessary to do it. But he was not bossy, and let her find out about the long hours herself and make her own decisions. That was the way a problem of Women's Lib was settled before World War I.
> —1982 interview with Bessie G. Murphy of Corvallis (born 1894, Elsie, Clatsop County)

Pickers at Meyer's hopyard with basket and sack for weighing, 1908

SOURCE: OHBA, OSU Special Collections and Archives Research Center, Corvallis, Oregon, Land Use Explorer, Gerald W. Williams Regional Albums (P 303). Identifier WilliamsG:GO

Rosa Cole on paying pickers:

A box of hops is supposed to weigh fifty pounds. That's when they got *fifty dollars* a box. That's what they thought they were paid, a cent a pound. Then, later on, they got to weighing them and paying them. I could tell you one incident of the way this A. Wolf, he brought his money in sacks, silver and gold, not paper, silver and gold. He sat down in a fence corner and laid his money out in front of him here and people went up and he figured how much he owed them and he paid them that. If it was three cents coming your way, you got a nickel. If it was three cents going his way, he got the nickel. He never paid any attention to pennies.

James Seavey Camp on the McKenzie River north of Springfield, Lane County, 1914

PHOTOGRAPHER: Smith Montjoy. SOURCE: Courtesy of the Lane County Historical Museum, SM244

In this photograph, the pickers' tents are in the foreground, with ranch buildings and barn in the background. Note the gardens on the right, bordered by stacked wood.

Alexander Seavey came to Oregon in 1850. In 1877 he began cultivating hops on twenty-five acres in Springfield along the McKenzie River, and ultimately the family was among the region's largest hop growers, with hopyards between Eugene and Portland. Alexander died in 1908 and his sons John, Jesse, and especially James continued and expanded the enterprise. By 1916 the J. W. Seavey Hop Company owned eight hundred acres and employed three thousand pickers. The Seavey camps advertised that they provided water, sawed wood, a table, and a grocery store and meat market on the premises.

The Seavey Company, along with the Horst Company, were not only growers, but also dealers, marketing and distributing their crop to brewers throughout the nation and to Europe.

Seavey pickers camp, 1914

PHOTOGRAPHER: Smith Montjoy. SOURCE: Courtesy of the Lane County Historical Museum, SM284

Note the Coburg Hills in the background of this photograph, the number of dryers, and the automobile parked behind tents on the left.

My mother and grandmother had picked hops together as we did, in the years when Seavey's ferry ran across the river to the hop yards. Whole families would camp out in the tents provided. I remember that too. Little cookstoves were in the tents, and one picker would leave earlier than the others to get supper started. They would cook real meals, no fast foods in those days. Appetites were hearty after all that work. After supper there'd be an hour or two of visiting and socializing by the older folks while the kids played in the twilight, for all the world like nobody was tired at all. And then the whole camp would settle down to slumber in those little tents. Dogs would bark, fires would go out. The old Mohawk River would furnish background murmurs for the sound of crickets and other night noises. And always the feel and the smell of the hops would be in my little girl dreams.

—1985 interview with M. E. Culver, Lane County Historical Museum

Campground on the Riverside hop farm, owned by A. J. Ray and Son, Inc., Newberg, Oregon, September 8, 1935

PHOTOGRAPHER: Al Monner © Thomas Robinson 2024

Some sense of the social character of these temporary communities is communicated through a sample of the material in 1925 issues of the *Hop Vine Scratch*, a newspaper produced by the Health and Recreation Service of the Lake Brook Hops Ranch of Salem. The publication was "Free to Hop Pickers" and published every other day during the September picking season.

Ladies Boxing Saturday Night. Ida Deering will compete with Alma Steimetz for the 115 lb. championship. Dorothy Johnson challenges any one of 95 to 100 lbs. Are there any others who would like to enter the ring!

Curly and Charlie, the "wire boys" of Section 1 were taking a wee nap in the rear seat of a car during noon hour Tuesday when Mrs. Schiffer stepped up and threw a small pail of water over them. Beware boys!

LOST: Light brown overcoat; Black pocket book with 50 cents and drivers licenses with name Elbert Flowers. Keep the 50 cents and return the rest.

PIE EATING CONTEST: Get your faces in shape for the pie eating contest, boys. You may be picked for it some evening next week. Louis Carpenter has a "Charlie Horse." He was not in best trim for game today. Perhaps that is why we lost.

WEDNESDAY NIGHT SHOW

Mr. C.A. Ryan gave several comic stories in Italian and Swedish dialect, all of which were much appreciated.

The contest was followed by some comic stories and a dramatic selection "The Shooting of Dan McGrew" by Mr. Jones. We all appreciated Mr. Jones' work, and are always glad to hear him.

Laura Kinsey played some selections on the accordion.

Walter and Martha Hemrich, 1915

SOURCE: Gerald W. Williams Regional Albums (P 303), OSU Special Collections and Archives Research Center, Corvallis, Oregon. Identifier WilliamsG:WV_children hops color

Lori Ryan spoke about her grandparents during an interview:

My grandfather, Walter Hemrich, was born in 1903 in Portland. His sister, Martha, was born in 1904. They resided at 1516 SE Pershing. Their parents were Adam Hemrich and Charlotte "Lottie" Schink-Hemrich. Walter and Martha picked hops routinely with their father and extended family.

Both Walter and Martha lived well into their eighties and always called Portland home. My grandfather had one daughter and three grandchildren. Martha never married. Walter worked as a warehouseman at EOFF electric for decades and Martha worked for the Oregon Society for the Blind. They were both very active in their Lutheran churches and were of German heritage.

Volga German pickers at German-owned hop field near St. Paul, 1920s

SOURCE: www.volgagermansportland and Kimberlee Henkel-Moody

In the eighteenth century Russia established a series of German colonies along the Volga River. In the 1870s many of the rights granted to the groups were withdrawn and the community sought to emigrate. In the 1880s large numbers settled in Portland, mostly in the Albina area.

Mollie Schneider Willman, a Volga German living in Portland's Albina neighborhood, reminisced about the summers she and her mother spent picking hops in the 1930s:

> The women cooked meals outside where wood-stoked cook stoves were situated, sometimes under an open-air shelter filled with picnic-style tables and benches. With no ice boxes available for cold storage, we would fill heavy bottles and containers with perishables (milk, for example) then seal them tightly and sink them in the creek. A truck from the local grocery came by every afternoon when the field work was finished, providing us with a veritable market on wheels. The driver sold fresh meat, eggs, and other groceries.

Pickers from the Grand Ronde Reservation, 1923

SOURCE: Oregon Historical Society, Folder Ag-Hops Wkrs., Neg. 65089

The Grand Ronde Reservation is located in the Grand Ronde Valley along the South Yamhill River in Yamhill and Polk Counties. On the eastern side of the coast range, it is in proximity to the major hop growing areas of the Willamette Valley. During the harvest season, it was common for tribal members to pick hops as well as other crops in the valley.

"Swedes" of Yamhill, circa 1900

SOURCE: Oregon Historical Society, Folder Ag-Hops Wkrs., Neg. 47370

Note the women wearing bonnets and the children and men wearing hats. Between 1880 and 1930, over forty thousand Swedes emigrated to Oregon.

Pickers near Independence

SOURCE: OHB, OSU Special Collections and Archives Research Center, Corvallis, Oregon, Willamette Basin Explorer, Land Use Explorer, Gerald W. Williams Regional Albums (P 303). Identifier WilliamsG:WV_hops Independence

"Yamhill—Miss Lela Murray of Yamhill County Schools, Plucks 1001 Pounds in Day and does it 'Clean.'

"Miss Lela Murray, a Yamhill County schoolteacher, on September 12 beat the former hop picking record by 170 pounds. Miss Murray picked 1001 pounds. She has a written statement from J.G. Morris for whom she picked, that these hops were picked clean and that there were no hops left on the ground or on the vines picked by her that day.

"This statement also gives the number of hours actually put in by Miss Murray in making this record picking as well as the weight of each of the sacks picked.

"These hops were picked entirely alone as the yard boss and Miss Murray would not allow anyone to help the young woman that day. In making the record Miss Murray used two baskets and kept up two rows alone.

"If she had been picking by the box this amount would be equivalent to about 21 boxes.

"Last year she made a record of 331 pounds in one day.

"Miss Murray has been a teacher in the school this year, near where she picked, for the past five years and is employed again this year."

—*Oregonian*, September 19, 1913

HOPS-INDEPENDENCE ORE.

Couple picking with dog

SOURCE: Oregon State Library

"Hop fields present one striking contrast to the city—there are no social barriers. Equality is maintained under the leveling action of the weighman's scales. For the man who weighs your hops is the man who decides your station. Preacher and bootblack, tradesman and farmer, factory hand and college boy, pick side by side. It does them all a world of good. That comradeship in the open air with the sun on their backs and sweat dripping from their foreheads.

"Natural competition under healthful conditions makes them man and man. The types one meets represent every shade of mankind. Here is a schoolteacher with a college degree, who is seeking health. Across from him is a town tramp earning money to buy beer. Here is the pretty daughter of a well-to-do farmer, the hops in her basket to pay for a pale pink party dress. A tired, nervous little woman is in the opposite row, with all the energy of her body in her work. She is raising a mortgage. There are boys whose earnings put them through college and others who are raising money to go to the devil. "

—*Oregonian*, 1907

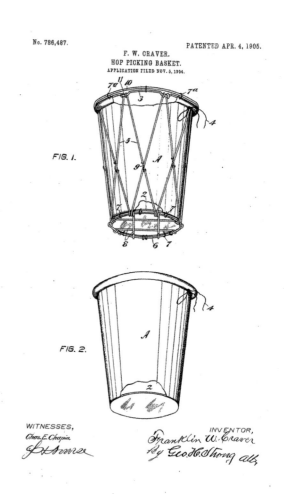

Craver hop patent

Pair of pickers, 1920s

SOURCE: Oregon State Library

"The words 'hop picking' are magic words for many because they signify to the grower that he is approaching the end of a long and weary season that involved hoeing, pruning, plowing, disking, staking, stringing, training, suckering, cultivating and spraying— not to mention threatened attacks of lice, spider and mildew, and the worries that go with these possibilities; and to the picker they mean several days of healthful outdoor employment and some much needed cash."

> —E. N. Bressman, Associate Professor of Farm Crops, Oregon State College
> and Agent of the United States Department of Agriculture, *Oregon Hop Grower*,
> September 1933

Pickers, Wigrich Ranch, 1928

SOURCE: Independence Heritage Museum

Wigrich Hop Ranch was located in Buena Vista, near Independence, Polk County. Wigrich was the largest hopyard under one trellis in the world during the 1920s. Started by the Krebs Brothers, the ranch was owned by an English company, Wigan, Richardson and Co. (hence its name). Mr. Wigan was an English brigadier general. Major W. Lewis Rose, a former English military officer experienced in English hopyards, managed the ranch. Wigrich's entire harvest went to the English market to be mixed with English hop, which were then seen as inferior. The October 5, 1913, Sunday *Oregonian* described the Wigrich campgrounds as a "model city" with a miniature street with stores, restaurants, large dance hall, a deputy sheriff on duty, with workers supplied campsites and wood, potatoes, and water. The ranch also had a large residence and "well-kept grounds decidedly English in their appearance." In the 1920s at picking time the ranch became a city of over one thousand. The ranch is now the site of Rogue Farms of Independence, which keeps the hop tradition alive.

Multigenerational pickers, Molalla, 1930

SOURCE: OHBA, OSU Special Collections and Archives Research Center, Corvallis, Oregon, Gerald W. Williams Collection. Identifier WilliamsG: WVgroupoutdoors

The experience of Martha Jane Nortz was typical of pickers from the local community. She picked from ages sixteen to nineteen in the 1930s.

I was raised in a large family so everyone helped out. We would get up around 5:00 a.m. and get the younger children dressed and ready for the day in the field. Have breakfast and pack a large lunch. Everyone had an idea of what they liked best, to eat, so there was quite a variety of sandwiches, fruits, and beverages to consider—we loaded into the old car by 6:00 a.m. and was on our way to the field. We made our work quite competitive to keep it interesting. We would generally take a fifteen-minute break around 9:30 or 10:00 a.m. then pick again until noon and do the same again until the p.m. Generally about an hour for lunch and rest. We usually would pick until 4 p.m. (or later) depending on how badly the crop need harvesting. When we got home there were baths to be taken and dinner to be cooked—many chores and cleaning to be done—we would go to bed, very tired but also thinking of another tiring and competitive day ahead. Even as young people, we made many friends from far and wide and looked forward to seeing them each day.

—Interview with Martha Jane Nortz, Independence (born 1922, Hale, Missouri)

Pickers with men on poles, 1930

SOURCE: Independence Heritage Museum, Wigrich Album

"Picking began yesterday at the big yards on the Wigrich hop ranch at Independence. Seven hundred pickers are employed. The yard contains nearly 400 acres, 30 acres being in fuggles. The Horst yards north of Independence also began picking this week, the early hops now being ready.

"It is reported from Harrisburg that hop picking began Monday on the Cartwright, Strods, Bennet and Bogs yards. Picking began last week at the Sam Fawyer yard. It is said that all the Harrisburg hops have been contracted. The yards mentioned above total more than 150 acres. Cartwright alone having nearly 100 acres."
—*Aurora Observer*, Marion County August 20, 1920. (The *Observer* was a weekly paper whose motto on the masthead read "The Sun Of Prosperity Shines On Aurora.")

Chinese pickers, Wigrich Ranch, 1930

SOURCE: Independence Heritage Museum

While growers and hopyard owners employed diverse groups of pickers, they had a clear preference for Caucasians. Referring to the character of the hop pickers at his hopyard in Fulton, just south of Portland, G. R. Stephenson said, "We have employed whites. All classes were represented among them—schoolteachers, book agents, bookkeepers, stenographers, clerks—and while we have had no ministers, we have had ministers' children. It keeps a good man hustling to pick five boxes of clean hops a day. I have seen girls up the valley pick as high as eight boxes a day, but it included a good many leaves and bits of vine" ("On a Model Hop Farm," *Oregonian*, October 6, 1895).

Twenty-seven years later there was a shortage of pickers and the *Independence Enterprise* (October 6, 1922) reported that "Major Lewis Rose, manager of the Wigrich ranch, has been forced to come to the conclusion that 'white help' cannot be depended upon to harvest hops."

Family of pickers, 1931

SOURCE: OHBA, OSU Special Collections and Archives Research Center, Corvallis, Oregon, Agricultural Experiment Station Records, 1889–2002 (RG 025)

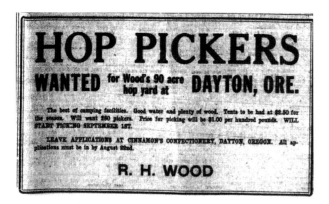

SOURCE: *Newberg Graphic,* August 3, 1922

Pickers, Wigrich Ranch, 1934

SOURCE: Oregon Historical Society, Folder Ag-Hop Wkrs.

Bessie Down picked hops from age eight until 1942. Her father was a field boss.

It wasn't hard work and it was fun, people sang, whistled, talked, yelled "wire down" and "box full" constantly. It was never dull. . . .

I think everyone around Independence in the late twenties and thirties looked forward to hop picking, even Baker's wives. . . .

Hop picking was a big event, the city (Independence) was small and it overflowed at that time, people came from everywhere to camp, our biggest yards was the "Wigrich" and Horst Ranch. I lived at Wigrich for thirteen years and worked all through the spring at the harvest. It was a very clean and beautiful campground. With a caretaker, sheriff, store, restaurant, meat market, and large area where people gathered at night around a campfire for entertainment.

—1982 interview with Bessie Down (born 1906, Independence)

WIGRICH RANCH
1934
Mr. RIGGS CHECK BOSS.

PHOTO.
ROBERT McEWAN
SALEM ORE.

Benedictine Sisters of Mount Angel Abbey picking hops, September 11, 1935

SOURCE: Oregon Historical Society, 000567

Mount Angel Abbey is a Benedictine community founded in 1882. It is the oldest seminary in the western United States. Hops have been grown at Mount Angel, where they do their own brewing, since its inception. In 2017 they opened a taproom for the sale of the products from the Benedictine Brewery.

Monks have produced beer for fifteen hundred years. St. Benedict envisioned monasteries as self-sufficient communities. In consequence, the Benedictines of the Middle Ages brewed in their own facilities, with their own labor, using ingredients grown on their own farms. The Benedictine Abbot Adalhard included the planting of hops in his set of instructions for his abbey in northern France in 1882. There is some debate about whether they were used for brewing.

Dorothea Lange, 1895–1965

PHOTOGRAPHER: Dorothea Lange. SOURCE: Library of Congress

Migratory boy, aged eleven, and his grandmother work side by side picking hops. Started work at five a.m. Photograph made at noon. Temperature 105 degrees. Oregon, Polk County, near Independence. Dorothea Lange, August 1939; Library of Congress, LC-USF34-020650-E [P&P] LOT 324.

Oregon, Josephine County, near Grants Pass. One room per family in rough wooden barracks on grower's property. No running water in camp. Hop ranch. Dorothea Lange, August 1939; Library of Congress, LC-USF34-020710-E [P&P] LOT 324.

Headed by Roy Stryker, the information division of the Farm Security Administration (FSA) had as its mission documenting the Depression experience of rural America to raise support for Franklin Roosevelt's New Deal programs. In this justifiably famous group, which included Walker Evans, Dorothea Lange was originally the only woman. She and her husband, the economist Paul Taylor, were often a documentary team—he wrote reports and she told the story through her photographs. The images were sociological documents that addressed the culture of rural and small-town life, paying particular attention to the plight of migrant laborers. Lange's photographs sympathetically humanized and personalized her subjects. Her work and that of the FSA are now recognized as great landmarks in the history of photography and many FSA images have become iconic, including Lange's most famous photo, *Migrant Mother*, taken in a migrant farmers camp in Nipomo, California.

Dorothea Lange, Picking hops

PHOTOGRAPHER: Dorothea Lange. SOURCE: Library of Congress

Oregon, Polk County, near Independence. Young wife of ex-logger, migratory field worker, picking hops. Dorothea Lange, August 1939; Library of Congress LC-USF34-020672-E [P&P] LOT 324.

Grower provides fourteen such shacks in a row for his hop pickers. Josephine County, Oregon. Near Grants Pass, Josephine County, Oregon. Dorothea Lange, August 1939; Library of Congress LC-USF34-021059-E.

Lange photographed hop pickers in Oregon while Russel Lee, another FSA photographer, did the same in Washington State. From August to October 1939, Dorothea Lange traveled through Oregon, Washington, and Idaho. The following are her notes from Polk County in August 1939.

Picking Hops

"Hop pickers start work in the field (called 'yard') with the first daylight and work until 5:30 in the late afternoon. Wages, 1 cent per pound of picker hops and the good pickers average about $1.50 per day.

"The hop is stripped from the vine, resembles a small green cone. The vine is lowered from the high wires over which it has been trained by the 'wire man' whose business is to bring the hops down to picking level. Hops are weighed in the yard and hauled to the kiln in sacks by truck. Negatives in this group were made at noontime, August 19, all in the same field. Temperature 105 degrees."

—Anne Whiston Spirn, *Daring to Look: Dorothea Lange's Photographs & Reports from the Field* (Chicago: University of Chicago Press, 2008)

Willamette Grocery Company of Salem, making a delivery to the Wigrich Ranch, 1930s

SOURCE: Independence Heritage Museum, 005

As a teenager in the 1930s, Beth Monroe managed her family's hop ranch while her father worked at the drier. She described it as not a very large operation near Independence that employed about one hundred pickers. She said that without access to transportation there were no stores nearby to purchase food.

So I had a little store ... probably ... maybe ten by twelve out of rough boards, with a window that would open up in the front. I had an icebox in it so I could go to town in the morning and get hamburger. That was what I usually got in the way of meat. I'd put it on ice and they'd have it that night for dinner. And then I could keep all kinds of canned foods. The bread man brought his bread truck into my store and sold me bread.

During the day, I had lots of soda pop too, and this was my best moneymaker. During the day I used my folk's car and I would load cold soda pop that I kept in a big tub with ice into the back of the car, in big wooden carriers that we had in those days ... glass bottles of soda pop ... and I'd take it out in the field where the people were picking hops. This was about the middle of the morning and middle of the afternoon, and everyone would come running, particularly the youngsters with their, I don't remember, I think it was probably a nickel that I was charging for it at that time. And they'd come running with their nickels and have just a little break while they drank their pop before they went back to picking hops.

Theater, Horst Ranch, near Independence, September 1, 1942

PHOTOGRAPHER: Al Monner © Thomas Robinson 5581

This photograph depicts the Lay's motion picture theatre tent at the hopyard at the E. Clemens Horst hop ranch near Independence on September 1, 1942. Advertising broadsides for upcoming films include two Castle war newsreels. These were only produced in 16 mm, which means that this theater used 16 mm projectors. The front canopy is probably twenty-four feet wide, and the main tent seating area is probably thirty-two by thirty-two with a sixteen-foot setback behind it for the screen. This size could easily be handled with a conventional bulb projector—probably a Bell & Howell Filmosound or something like it—rather than carbon arc. Signs advertise a vaudeville stage show for the evening, with a magic show and a "self-supporting baby."

Kids' camp area, Horst ranch, 1942

PHOTOGRAPHER: Al Monner © Thomas Robinson

Hop historian Peter Kopp characterized Emil Clemons Horst (1867–1940) as the "Pacific Coast's quintessential hop dealer." A German immigrant, Horst moved west as a child. His first hopyards were in California and proved enormously successful. He then expanded his operations into Oregon in the vicinity of Independence. Ultimately 10 percent of Oregon's hops were from Horst properties. On September 3, 1915, the *Independence Monitor* proclaimed that the Clemens Horst ranch, known locally as the Eola ranch, was the world's largest at 567 acres with 1250–1500 pickers that year and a picking machine. Six years later, on August 12, 1921, the *Independence Enterprise* reported that the Eola ranch was still the world's largest at 1,081 acres. The article added that "the fields present a beautiful sight, the growth heavy, and acre after acre is spread before the eye." The Eola ranch introduced progressive services for pickers. It provided tents, sanitation, water, and fuel. It also had a camp newspaper, concessions, and an active recreation program with playgrounds, campfires, dances, and religious programs.

In addition, the Horst Company was responsible for many innovations. It was perhaps the first to use a high trellis system, sometimes called "The California System" in Oregon. It also introduced changes to the construction and mechanisms used in kilns and cooling barns that were widely adapted. In 1909 the company patented a mechanical hop harvester and Edouard Thys, E. Clemens Horst's son-in-law, invented the portable picker in 1937.

Braceros weighing, 1942

SOURCE: OHBA, OSU Special Collections and Archives Research Center, Corvallis, Oregon, Extension Bulletin Illustrations Photograph Collection, 1915–1963 (P 020). Identifier P20_1981

Carl Ehlen, a yard boss, describes the weighing process:

> We used spring scales hanging at the top of three poles. There was a bolt thorough the top ends of the three poles with sacks hanging on bolt. You could spread the bottom of the poles attach the sack of hops to hook on scales then take the middle pole, push it so the three pole legs were closer together. This would lift the sack of hops off the ground and give weight of sack on scales—the boss punched out weight and ticket and gave same to the hop picker. The yard boss also checked the hops to see they did not put in clods or too many stems and leaves.
> —1982 interview with Carl Ehlen (born 1904, near Hubbard)

Bracero workers, 1943

SOURCE: OHBA, OSU Special Collections and Archives Research Center, Corvallis, Oregon, Harriet's Photograph Collection, 1868–1996 (P HC). Identifier HC2969

With most able-bodied men in the service during World War II, there was an acute home-front labor shortage. To partially fill the gap, the federal government authorized the bracero program in 1942. In the Farm Labor Agreement between the United States and Mexico, workers were brought largely to do maintenance work and agricultural labor. The name "bracero," from the Spanish *brazo* (arm), clearly defined the fact that the men were manual laborers. The workers were mostly young men from rural backgrounds, and few spoke English. Ultimately half a million workers came between 1941 and 1947; forty-seven thousand would work in the Pacific Northwest. (The program expanded as a guest workers program; its extension lasted until 1964.)

Under the agreement the men were guaranteed prevailing wages, health care, adequate housing, and board. At the local level, the program was administered by Oregon State College (now Oregon State University). For braceros, hop picking was a short-term enterprise; they joined the community of hop pickers for the duration of the harvest and then returned to other agricultural labor, predominantly harvesting fruits and vegetables. For most workers it was a positive experience despite being so far from home. Growers needed and appreciated their hard work, and in some camps, they joined in the evening's entertainment. However, in some hopyards the living conditions were poor and braceros experienced discrimination in surrounding communities. Though the agreement specified that braceros were temporary workers and were required to return to Mexico, an unknown number remained or returned as unauthorized immigrants, ultimately becoming members of the state's Mexican American community.

In this photograph, Humberto Videl Garcia, interpreter, receives instruction from Jack Hardwicke, crew chief.

Women's Land Army, 1942

SOURCE: OHBA, OSU Special Collections and Archives Research Center, Corvallis, Oregon Harriet's Photograph Collection, 1868–1996 (P HC). Identifier HC0972

On the home front during World War II there was a critical labor shortage, especially in farming communities. Congress created the Women's Land Army—modeled after the Women's Land Army of America (WWLA) from World War I—to support the war effort, and from 1943 to 1945, thousands of women were recruited and trained as agricultural workers. These women were the rural counterpart of Rosie the Riveter. Ultimately 3.5 million women nationally participated in the WLA, with seventy-eight thousand in Oregon. The women had to be at least eighteen years old and physically fit, but farm experience was not required. In this photo you see two WLA members wearing the official (but optional) WLA uniform of blue denim overalls and powder-blue shirts. Florence Hall was the national director and Mabel Mack, Oregon State College (OSC) extension nutritionist, supervised the WLA in Oregon. Historians credit women's work during the war as a watershed in the history of the women's movement, as they amply proved their capacities in fields and occupations previously occupied almost exclusively by men.

Co-eds with hoes, 1945

SOURCE: OHBA, OSU Special Collections and Archives Research Center, Corvallis, Oregon, Harriet's Photograph Collection, 1868–1996 (P HC). Identifier HC0972

Co-ed is a short form of coeducational, in reference to institutions educating men and women. It was first used in the 1870s after previously male-only institutions admitted women. The term later assumed its meaning of exclusively female students, typically young, attending a college or university. The term, sometimes used in a derogatory fashion, is now archaic. During the home-front labor shortages of World War II, college co-eds were "drafted" to do agricultural work.

Oregon State University, incorporated as Corvallis College, admitted women since its inception. Its first graduating class of three in 1870 included Alice E. Biddle, who graduated at age sixteen with a bachelor of science degree.

The co-eds in the photograph were members of the Alpha Lambda Delta Sorority. Left to right they are Alice Root, Mary Lou George, Marie Hansen, Ruby Carlos, Shirley Young, and Margaret Eefsen. They were working at the college's hop farm.

In the 1940s when this photo was taken, "hop" was also the term for a dance and the most popular dance was the Lindy Hop. According to some sources, the term derived from dances done at hop festivals in the Midwest when the region, especially Milwaukee, was the center of beer brewing in the United States.

Soldiers from Camp Adair picking hops, 1944

SOURCE: OHBA, OSU Special Collections and Archives Research Center, Corvallis, Oregon, Agriculture Photograph Collection, ca. 1890–1970 (P 040). Identifier P40_0146

Camp Adair was located six miles north of Corvallis in the center of the state's hops-growing region. Opened in 1942, it ultimately housed thirty-five thousand personnel over fifty-five thousand acres, making it the second biggest "city" in the state during World War II. To create the camp, land was requisitioned, the small town of Wells was abandoned, and even cemeteries were removed. Almost eighteen hundred structures were built, including barracks, hospital, movie theaters, and even full-scale models of European and Japanese towns for training purposes. Over one hundred thousand soldiers received their training there. In 1943 soldiers at the camp were "drafted" to help in the hops harvest. From 1944 to 1946 the camp was repurposed as a prisoner of war (POW) camp for Italian and German prisoners. They were also put to work harvesting hops and other crops in the area. After the war the camp was abandoned and all but two buildings were demolished, sold, or moved.

Cutting down vines for the picking machine, E. Clemens Horst ranch near Independence, 1942

Dorothy Schriever remembered working on one of the first portable picking machines in the area from from 1949 to 1951, for which she was paid one dollar an hour:

> At first I worked in one of the "crow's nests" at the front of the portable picking machine, cutting the vines off of the top vine (they had already been cut by another person on the ground) and swinging the end of the vine around to the person on the clamp to clamp the vine to proceed through the machine. Some of the vines were very heavy so because of this I later switched to the clamps and also rotated to the belt, picking out leaves. But mostly I either worked in the "crow's nest" or on the clamps. One two-week period I drove the caterpillar tractor which pulled the portable picking machines. This was the most difficult of all for me as the clutch had to be engaged at every hop hill—or about every eight feet down the row, and had to be engaged very gradually so as not to jerk workers on machine. This took tremendous leg muscle control in my left leg and I was glad when that two weeks was over. When we worked on the portable hop-picking machine, we worked eight-hour shifts at night because the hops picked better with the machine at night. If it was cool weather, they would run it during the day with a day shift too.
> —1982 interview with Dorothy Schriever (born 1935, Hubbard)

On September 14, 1915, the *Polk County Observer* reported that hundreds of visitors came to witness the new hop-picking machine at the E. Clement Horst Company hopyards. It was described as "a modern wonder, produced by the inventive ingenuity of Mr. Horst himself." The machine did not pick in the fields as later picking machines would do, but vines were hauled to the machines, where a series of cylinders separated the hop from the vines.

Hauling over two tons of bales on wagon, 1880

SOURCE: Or.Digital-df71gw58c

Well, my uncle was one of the firemen for drying the hops. I was involved in that I would empty them off the kiln and dump them in the storehouse. Then we'd leave them in there and when it was time to get the storehouse unloaded, it was all done (through picking and everything—they were dried and cured), why we'd start baling. Me and the boss's son, were the two balers. Of course we had three of them when we had the horse. Had a team of horses that pulled the plunger down. Why then you had three. Just took two of us to run off the electrical operated baler. We'd handle them, finish up the bale, sew it all up, and store it over at the warehouse. Then when it was all through, we'd haul them to Salem. . . .

They probably did it by wagon before my time. I drove an old Model A truck and had a V8 truck, too. Had two different trucks that we hauled them with. Had quite a load on them. I forget how many bales we used to have on there. I know there were about as high as the ceiling anyway. So we had a pretty good load of hops on there.

—1982 interview with Tom Kraemer (born 1918, Mt. Angel)

Liles Hop House, Lane County near Junction City or Crow area, 1895

SOURCE: Oregon Historical Society, Folder Ag-Hops Wkrs., 12190

In the photograph, Milt Lile loads bags of hops via a wooden slide while Jim Inman stands nearby. Hops were stored in the barn loft.

"S. Smeed of Walterville, Dried 5,000 Pounds of Prunes in his Hop House
"Stephen Smeed of Waterville, after finishing his hop crop, utilized his hop house in drying prunes, and from the samples shown, he has done as good work as the average fruit dryer, constructed specially for the purpose.

"In order to use the hop house for drying fruit no change was made except to change the cloth on the top hop floor. At first a thin coating of the fruit was laid on the floor, but after a few hours it was gathered together about three inches in thickness. It took him about ten hours longer to dry a flooring than the regular evaporators.

"He paid sixty cents per 100 pounds for the green Italian prunes, and purchased all offered at that price. He has about 5000 pounds of the dried article produced thusly.

"It is likely that many hop houses will hereafter be used for drying fruit after the hop crop is turned off."
—*Eugene City Guard*, October 2, 1897

Pickers loading sacks onto a horse-drawn wagon, 1914

SOURCE: Oregon Historical Society, Folder Ag-Hops Wkrs., 12190

In his Pulitzer–Prize winning novel, *Honey in the Horn* (1935), H. L. Davis described the experience of hop pickers in the first decade of the twentieth century.

"There was plenty of sportiveness and high spirits around the hop-fields that fall. Hops were fetching thirty-five cents a pound at the drier, and the hundred-acre patch where they were camped stood to return its owner a profit of sixty thousand dollars, clear of all expenses for planting, plowing, poling, stringing, picking, drying, and baling. The owner walked around between the rows, looking solemn and responsible about it, though that may have been due to his wearing his best clothes, including a stiff-bosomed shirt and a funeral-model stand-up collar. His hops were going to make him rich, and since they couldn't be cashed in on till they got picked, he felt bound to tog himself out uncomfortably by way of showing his pickers how much he appreciated their being there. He had even taken care to see that everybody got camped decently. All the campsites were laid off with shade, clean water, brick fireplaces, straw for bedding, and free clotheslines out in the open pastures where the women could hang their washing. There was a small commissary store handling fresh meat and common groceries and gloves and work clothes. . . ." (p. 150)

"The hop-field had seemed a place where people minded their own business and let one another alone, but it wasn't any such thing. It was a good like an inquisitive-minded village, that had kept its identity, its social levels, and its inquisitiveness unaltered through all the moving around it did in the course of the year." (p. 160)

NO 597-X- PICKING HOPS IN OREGON.

Hop baskets

SOURCE: Independence Heritage Museum, img_6251

"G. F. Mason writes from Salem, Ore., that business is good there, though he laments there are not more factories in the city. Mr. Mason is the head of G. F. Mason Co. which manufactures hop baskets, fruit dryer trays, boxes, berry crates and step ladders."
    —*The Barrel and Box*, trade journal (Chicago), 1905

"C. D. Edwards of the Portland Fruit and Hop Basket Co. is promoting the establishment of a basket factory in Hillsboro, Ore."
    —*The Barrel and Box*, trade journal (Chicago), 1905

"The chief product of this factory [Portland Manufacturing Company in the St. Johns area of Portland] consists of coffee and spice barrels, 'draw bottoms,' furniture stock and veneer, coffee drums and splint baskets, fruit baskets and hop picking baskets. . . . In the single article of hop picking baskets it turns out between 450 and 500 dozen in a season and the number is increasing rapidly."
    —*St. Johns Review,* January 13, 1905

The J. E. Krauger Hop Basket Company in Salem from 1928 to 1948 specialized in making wooden hop baskets, but also provided hops scoops and quassia wood chips.

Weighing a bale of hops

SOURCE: Josephine County Historical Society

I've done everything from picking hops, to baling them, to hauling them to the Salem breweries where they used to make Salem beer.

Each bale would weigh around two or three hundred pounds . . . at least three hundred pound. Take a lot of hops to make one bale of hops. I forget how many scoops it took, but it was quite a few. The scoop had roller wheels on it on the bottom, wooden rollers, canvas around the sides. You'd run that into the hops, tip it back by hand, and take it over to the baler and push it into the baler. The baler was about twelve foot high or better, I guess. Compress that down to about three feet to get the right amount of hops in one bale—you have to do that. Then samplers would come along and they would take a pound sample out of a bale every once in a while to see if they were acceptable to the brewery, to sell them. They were lucky all the time, they always sold most of all their hops. Course, they didn't get an awful lot for them, but they got pretty good money.

—Tom Kraemer

Bales of surplus hops used for fertilizer, 1934

PHOTOGRAPHER: Ben Maxwell. SOURCE: Oregon Historical Society, 020067

In the midst of the Depression, the government paid seven dollars a bale for surplus bags of hops not sold to brewers in 1934—a fraction of their costs, and of the forty cents a pound brewers normally paid.

"Hopyard near Wheatland, ten miles north of Salem, is being fertilized with 575 bales of 1934 hops. This is a government measure for relieving hop surpluses and restringing better prices for hop growers. If the growers could have sold at this year's top price they would have received approximately $45,000. Now, with hops selling for less than production cost, the government is paying growers $7 a bale for old bags used as orchard or hopyard fertilizer."
—*Pacific Hop Grower*, April 1938

Group photo drier and kiln, 1893

SOURCE: Oregon Historical Society, Folder Ag-Hops Wkrs.

I remember one time there was a whole bunch of us young people. This was on a Sunday or something, so we went to the hop house and went upstairs and went in the kiln. The floors were in slats like this, and they had a very thin cloth stretched over this where they laid the hops. They were about three feet deep, I think, they would lay these hops, and then these stoves underneath. They built the fires in these stoves and they put sulfur pots on there to bleach the hops. They had taken the hops out of the kiln and it was still warm in there. There was one girl, and this fellow was very jealous of her, and there was another fellow went with her that day, and we went up there. He went up and shut this door and put this sulfur pot on that stove. Well, it just about killed one, that girl. If it hadn't have been my brother was with us to finally force that door open, she would have died from suffocation from that sulfur.

—Rosa Cole

Lowell kiln and dryer, 1899

SOURCE: OHBA, OSU Special Collections and Archives Research Center, Corvallis, Oregon, Willamette Basin Explorer, Land Use Explorer. Identifier WilliamsG:SWV Lowell hophouse

Al Hansen, whose family opened a hopyard in 1925, describes day-to-day activities:

A check boss and two helpers would weigh the hops after putting them in sacks and punch the tickets. A sack buck (he would throw the full sacks in the wagon). The field boss was in charge of seeing that all this was done usually in teams and drivers they would haul them. Sacked hops to the dryer. At the dryer three men would unload the wagons by the kilns. This was done by dumping the hops on an elevated floor twenty feet from the ground, burlap covered to blow the heat to get to the hops. The fireman would start the fire in the furnace that burned four foot wood. After drying the hops for fourteen to eighteen hours they would be dry and ready to shove off into the cooling room to cool off the baled into 200-pound bales. The pickers received from $0.80 cents a hundred pounds to $1.50. It differed from year to year. The day workers received from twenty cents an hour to seventy-five here. It also varied from year to year. We received seven cents a pound to eighteen cents. The hops dried away four to one for every four pounds of green hops they dried to one pound, so no one made much money.

—1982 interview with Al Hansen

SOURCE: Independence Heritage Museum, Wigrich Album

Marty Martin March describes picking hops when she was in her twenties:

After the day's picking the men would haul hop in sacks to the hop house drive on a platform "sorta" of runway to the hop dryer door, where they were unloaded, taken into the kiln room which had a slatted floor, dumped on the floor, and an experienced man if possible would lay the floor or hops on the floor, which was very important as if they wasn't laid right were very hard to dry evenly, if they wasn't laid even all over floor sometimes some would have to be sort of stirred up or leveled out to dry better after they were dried. They had large hop "scoops" or sorta shovels made of some lumber and burlap and dumped into hop bin. After they got a floor or two in the bin it was very dangerous in bin room for man to walk on and dump scoop on either side. If he fell in, he was quite liable to die as no one could get to him. Those hops were a bit like "feathers"—you didn't dare to try to dog anyone out or you'd be gone too. I've known a few that did suffocate in the bin.

   —1982 interview with Marty Martin March (born 1894, Atwood, Kansas)

On main street of a Willamette Valley town, Independence, Polk County, Oregon, August 1939

PHOTOGRAPHER: Dorothea Lange. SOURCE: Library of Congress, LC-USF34- 020639-E [P&P] LOT 32

The Hop Fiesta (note sign and poster in the photograph) began as the three-day Hops Festival in late summer in 1934. The festival was located at the Hop Bowl, a Public Works Administration (PWA) project seating four thousand people. The festival included a parade with floats, the crowning of a Hop Queen, fireworks, games, carnival, boxing matches, a rodeo, dances, and amateur and vaudeville performances. The festival ended in the 1950s with the decline of hops production in the area. The festival was revived in 2001 as the Independence Hop and Heritage Festival.